Blessings *and* Prayers *for* Married Couples

Blessings *and* Prayers *for* Married Couples

A Faith Full Love

ISABEL ANDERS

Liguori
LIGUORI, MISSOURI

Imprimi Potest: Thomas D. Picton, CSsR
Provincial, Denver Province, The Redemptorists

Published by Liguori Publications
1 Liguori Drive, Liguori, Missouri 63057
To order, call 800-325-9521 or visit www.liguori.org.

Library of Congress Cataloging-in-Publication Data

Anders, Isabel, 1946-
    Blessings and prayers for married couples: a faith full love / Isabel Anders—
1st ed.
    p. cm.
    ISBN 978-0-7648-1933-9 (hard cover with jacket)
    1. Spouses—Prayers and devotions. 2. Catholic Church—Prayers and devo-
tions. I. Title.

BX2170.M3A53 2011
242'.644—dc22

                                                                2010049159

Additional copyright acknowledgments are in the Acknowledgments section.

Liguori Publications, a nonprofit corporation, is an apostolate of the Redemptorists.
To learn more about the Redemptorists, visit Redemptorists.com.

Printed in the United States of America
15 14 13 12 11   5 4 3 2 1
First edition

To my husband, Bill,
with love and gratefulness.

"If ever two were one, then surely we. If ever man were loved by wife, then thee."

—ANNE BRADSTREET (C. 1612–1672)

I would like to thank my longtime agent Tracy Grant,
without whose efforts and encouragement "above and beyond,"
this book would not have been possible.

Contents

How to Use This Book

*We do not believe in formulas, but in those realities they
express, which faith allows us to touch.*
—*CATECHISM OF THE CATHOLIC CHURCH*

How can a book of prayers bring us closer to God and to
one another? On their own, a book and the words in
it are mere tools. A book can sit on a coffee table or a
shelf and simply indicate that the people in the household have
this specific concern and even plan to read about it sometime!
A prayer book can be well worn, opened frequently, and used
as a guide on occasions when praying together is unarguably
the right response in the moment—whether it takes the form
of a solemn duty, a desperate cry, or a loving conversation
that may be extended and repeated throughout the years and
decades of married life.

Some of the approaches, prayers, and topics in this book
will resonate more than others within the patterns of a couple's
life together.

And attitude matters. Simply deciding to sit down, designate
a spot, and make a time to pray together as a married couple
is *an act of choice*. It is a matter of inviting God to meet us in
our routines and in our intentions to live in "faith full love"
together—to experience the continuing flow of God's grace

as a couple and as individuals, often as parents and workers and citizens as well, since many of the key principles of living embodied in these prayers carry over to our "other" lives in wider community.

Choosing to plant and grow and nurture a "faith full love" is a life-changing choice—a choice that provides an opening for God to work in specific, powerful ways in your marriage, in your family, and in your future.

Therefore these prayers and perspectives, based on the seven lines of the marriage vow, can be seen as "openings on the eternal." Some are formal and poetic, others are practical and plainspoken. But all are presented as potential guides for naturally incorporating prayer into a marriage: making praying together a priority, choosing it as a focal point among the many options pulling at us in our busy, demanding lives.

Voices both ancient and modern are to be found in these pages. Collected from various sources through the centuries, they speak in various ways—each adding different aspects of concern, shades of admonition, points of praise—that together offer ways to consider marriage and faithfulness in light of the larger issues facing us in the Christian life.

The questions and thoughts included in the sections of this book are intended to expand the experiences of couples' prayer times—to lead to discussion and action, healing and ministry, along whatever paths the pray-ers are called to follow.

It is a privilege and a joy to present *Blessings and Prayers for Married Couples: A Faith Full Love* with these hopes and prayers in mind.

ISABEL ANDERS
SEWANEE, TENNESSEE

Introduction

A Faith Full Love

It is love that asks, that seeks, that knocks, that finds, and that is faithful to what it finds.

—SAINT AUGUSTINE OF HIPPO

The first form of communion between persons is that born of the love of a man and a woman who decide to enter a stable union in order to build together a new family.

—POPE BENEDICT XVI

By wisdom a house is built, and by understanding it is established.

—PROVERBS 24:3

For where two or three are gathered in my name, I am there among them.

—MATTHEW 18:20

The experience of married couples' praying together, intentionally and joyfully, offers one of the greatest opportunities for hope and unity at the core of family life. Regular prayer times allow *any* married couple—of a few days, years, or decades—to stay in intimate touch, not only with God and God's purposes for them, but with each other's heart and soul.

Agreeing to enter into prayer—at appointed times of the day, at meals, at bedtime, and at family events—can be an ongoing, fulfilling practice.

Jesus admonished his followers to pray at all times and "not to lose heart" (Luke 18:1). Yet Christian prayer goes far beyond positive thinking and even "possibility thinking." When we pray we enter into a rich, ancient tradition and ongoing practice of imploring God to join with us in our human longing and desire for God's own kingdom to "come."

In the First Letter of Paul to the Thessalonians, we are encouraged to "pray without ceasing" (5:16). This can only be referring to an attitude toward God that extends deep into the soul and to a receptive spirit that rises to spoken prayer when appropriate. We are not expected to be on our knees or addressing God at all times—but rather to incorporate prayer into our lives in such a way that praying and praising are never out of possibility in the moment, no matter our circumstances.

True prayer can also reveal God's wisdom to us. In the Letter of James, we are told that through an attitude of receptivity, we will be given true insight "generously and ungrudgingly" by the God who holds us in love (1:5).

But prayer can have practical, tangible effects in our daily lives as well as we position our bodies and minds to seek God together on a regular basis.

I've seen surveys in which the practice of praying together was shown to be the strongest factor in predicting a long-term marriage. Partners who prayed together had a divorce rate of just 1 percent. It stands to reason, since being able to pray together implies being somewhat, at least, "on the same page."

But to talk first about this effect of prayer on its practitioners is really to put the cart before the horse. The fellowship of couples' prayer, like all spiritual disciplines, is not about prevention or remedy. It is at first, perhaps, a duty we undertake regularly—even when we don't feel like it. But in the surrender that is prayer, we learn first simply to be there—and then to "let go" and let God do the rest. We can then prepare to be astonished and nurtured and held by the One who has brought us together in the first place.

True prayer—putting flesh on the "bones" of spiritual practice—emerges naturally, spontaneously, out of the quality of the relationship that undergirds it. And so talking about prayer in marriage necessarily involves much more than tips on technique, frequency, and the virtue of discipline. The prayers spouses can offer together arise primarily out of the context of commitment and love that surrounds and shelters both partners—while allowing for personal, respectful freedom of two separate, individual wills:

- When our spouse is the first person with whom we long to share any news, good or bad, such that an experience or event is "incomplete" without his or her reception and input—this is fertile ground for true prayer.

- When our heart sincerely longs for the spiritual well-being of our partner in any and all situations, we have grasped the basis of a partnership-in-love that underlies genuine prayer.

- When our joy and grief—and all the other spontaneous responses to real life—naturally find expression along with our partner's as intentional mutual offerings to God...joint prayer is being experienced, whether words are actually said or not.

This book follows the vows couples take initially—but focuses especially on ways to renew these ideals through the stages of ongoing marriage. It uses a "grammar" of love that chooses positive verbs—love, listen, care, give, share, support —and skillfully directs them toward the agreed-upon object: you, thou, my beloved-the spouse, the other.

Even as we become more proficient in the language of exchange, of selflessness, of surrender—in some ways we will always remain beginners. Yet we will also find ourselves growing in stages to experience greater commitment, doubled joy, and more secure grounding in the life of the Spirit that is prayer.

Some of the principles and practices will be more helpful or fitting than others; and some may prove appropriate at different stages or at future points on your journey. But all are offered to enhance the adventure and the challenge of "two becoming one" as Jesus envisioned it.

Who can say how two become one? Prayer is only part of the equation. But when couples experience a deeper unity on this level, prayer is certainly the appropriate response to the mystery—a thankfulness to the God of love.

When Two
Are One

"I take you to be my spouse"

"…and the two shall become one flesh." So they are no longer two, but one flesh.

—MARK 10:8

There is nothing nobler or more admirable than when two people who see eye to eye keep house as man and wife, confounding their enemies and delighting their friends.

—HOMER

Let marriage be held in honor by all, and let spouses remain faithful to one another.

—PARAPHRASE OF HEBREWS 13:4

In the wedding rite, the true purpose of marriage is revealed most sacredly and succinctly when two people, before God and many witnesses, vow to each other, "I take you to be my spouse."

The poet W. H. Auden wrote, "Like everything which is not the involuntary result of fleeting emotion but the creation of time and will, any marriage, happy or unhappy, is infinitely more interesting than any romance, however passionate."

Interesting? Yes. Easy? Hardly ever. Marriage requires an initial, deliberate choice as well as ongoing effort to sustain this living-in-unity—through the years of working out what such a commitment means—in everyday ways and within the larger scope of married life.

Any true marriage is, in the catchy phrase of author Madeleine L'Engle, a "two-part invention." For Christian men and women, becoming one with each other will always involve Another. In his First Letter to the Corinthians, Saint Paul says, "Do you not know that your body is a temple of the Holy Spirit within you, which you have from God, and that you are not your own? For you were bought with a price; therefore glorify God in your body" (6:19–20).

We belong to God, and so our lives are not simply *ours* to give; they are also God's. And in the marriage vow before God, this transaction, this *giving*, takes place as we acknowledge *mystery*—two becoming one, with God's blessing.

The Christian marriage vow, "I take you to be my spouse," is not merely a one-time affirmation, said in the midst of flowers and friends on a perfectly orchestrated day. That is the sacramental and public aspect of the vow. But the desire for fidelity in marriage, blessed by God, is an inner decision that begins well before the ceremony. And that same commitment is needed to sustain and strengthen the partners in this unique union of bodies and souls as it is lived out, day by day, thereafter.

As Jesuit John S. Dunne writes in his book *The Reasons of the Heart,* "If I set my heart upon another person, then I cannot live without that person. My heart becomes divided. On the other hand, if I give my life to the journey with God, then my heart becomes whole and I can be whole in a relationship with another."

Christian spirituality teaches us that genuine love of God is the best formula for being able to love others, including our beloved. When we give our heart to God, we begin to experience the healing and wholeness that allow our love to expand rather than contract. Although we will give our love in exclusive ways to our marriage partner, we will also be enabled—as individuals and as a couple—to love beyond our boundaries in ways that draw others in rather than shutting them out.

And so, how will we celebrate our vows—and learn to live them—not only on the day of our wedding but through the days and years of our marriage? The following prayers and blessings give voice to some of the beauties and challenges that await.

Thoughts, Prayers, and Blessings

FIRST, WE REMEMBER:

Father, you have made the bond of marriage a holy mystery, a symbol of Christ's love for his Church.

Hear our prayers for [N.] and [N]. With faith in you and in each other, they pledge their love today. May their lives always bear witness to the reality of that love. We ask you this through our Lord Jesus Christ, your Son, who lives and reigns with you and the Holy Spirit, one God, for ever and ever. Amen.

—OPENING PRAYER FOR CATHOLIC WEDDING

AND WE TRUST GOD FOR THE KEEPING OF THESE VOWS:

[In this ___ year of our marriage/on this anniversary], may God bless us and grant us joy. May God deepen our love for each other. May God bless us through our family and friends, and lead us to unending happiness in heaven.

May Almighty God, Father, Son, and Holy Spirit, shower favor on us all, and keep us in God's love for ever and ever. Amen.

—TRADITIONAL PRAYER ADAPTED

I'm glad I'm married, Lord, but it isn't always easy. Help us then, Lord, to say what is on our hearts and minds in a way that the other can hear. And help each of us to listen. Give me patience, Lord, when I should be patient and courage to speak out in disagreement when it is important. And remind me to do those little things which sometimes make all the difference.

—AVERY BROOKE IN *PLAIN PRAYERS IN A COMPLICATED WORLD*

May you be graced with God's presence
and gifted with God's grace.
May the Holy Spirit enlighten and enliven you,
and may the love of Christ sustain you.
Long after your wedding day is over,
may the days of your marriage be joyous and rich.
May you find shelter and safety in each other's arms,
respect and reverence in each other's eyes,
and a home in each other's heart.
May your friendship be faithful and firm, your trust total.
And may you remain young at heart as you grow old together.
May God bless you…and we do, too.
Amen.

—WILLIAM E. RABIOR AND SUSAN C. RABIOR IN
9 WAYS TO NURTURE YOUR MARRIAGE

Love is patient, love is kind.
It does not envy, it does not boast,
it is not proud. It does not dishonor others,
it is not self-seeking,
it is not easily angered,
it keeps no record of wrongs.
Love does not delight in evil but rejoices with the truth.
It always protects, always trusts,
always hopes, always perseveres.
Love never fails.…
And now these three remain: faith, hope and love.
But the greatest of these is love.

—1 CORINTHIANS 13, *NEW INTERNATIONAL VERSION*

My heart overflows with a goodly theme;
I address my verses to the king;
my tongue is like the pen of a ready scribe.

You are the most handsome of men;
grace is poured upon your lips;
therefore God has blessed you forever.

Gird your sword on your thigh,
O mighty one,
in your glory and majesty.

In your majesty ride on victoriously
for the cause of truth and to defend the right;
let your right hand teach you dread deeds.
Your arrows are sharp in the heart of the king's enemies;
the peoples fall under you.

Your throne, O God, endures forever and ever.
Your royal scepter is a scepter of equity;
you love righteousness and hate wickedness.
Therefore God, your God, has anointed you
with the oil of gladness beyond your companions;
your robes are all fragrant with myrrh and aloes and cassia.
From ivory palaces stringed instruments make you glad;
daughters of kings are among your ladies of honor;
at your right hand stands the queen in gold of Ophir.

Hear, O daughter, consider and incline your ear;
forget your people and your father's house,
and the king will desire your beauty.
Since he is your lord, bow to him;

the people of Tyre will seek your favor with gifts,
the richest of the people with all kinds of wealth.

The princess is decked in her chamber with gold-woven robes;
in many-colored robes she is led to the king;
behind her the virgins, her companions, follow.
With joy and gladness they are led along
as they enter the palace of the king.

In the place of ancestors you, O king, shall have sons;
you will make them princes in all the earth.
I will cause your name to be celebrated in all generations;
therefore the peoples will praise you forever and ever.

—PSALM 45

Now you will feel no rain,
for each of you will be shelter for the other.
Now you will feel no cold,
for each of you will be warmth to the other.
Now there will be no loneliness,
for each of you will be companion to the other.
Now you are two persons, but there are three lives before you:
his life, her life, and your life together.
Go now to your dwelling place to enter into your days together.
And may all your days be good and long upon the Earth.

—POPULAR WEDDING BLESSING

In the symphony of your concord and love, the praises of Jesus
Christ are sung.

—SAINT IGNATIUS OF ANTIOCH (C. 35–107)

While it is important that we do not disregard the literal level of Psalm 45, it is not inappropriate for us also to think of the traditional image of God's union with his people as a kind of wedding. We are, in this day, quite wary of the dangers of flowery allegorization, the assumption that we can make a one-for-one identification of each detail with some hidden "spiritual" meaning. Yet we can certainly say that any wedding can tell us something about God's love....

The deeper we penetrate the mystery of romantic imagery, aware of both its usefulness and its limitations, the more we seem to be talking with an urgent but dying breath. To speak of the union of heaven and earth—or of any true union of opposites at all when the world is impossibly broken, splintered, can seem naive at best.

But the application of the sexual metaphor of marriage does have a long history. It is found in some of the greatest poetry in the Christian tradition from the Song of Solomon onward, and helps to balance the Christian tradition of celibacy, so closely associated with pure devotion and dedication to spiritual ideals.

Both the union of bodies in marriage and the denial of sexual intimacy in the celibate condition can point to God as the giver of all good things, including the body and its potential for service. The Apostle Paul writes of marriage as an analogy of Christ's love for the Church (Ephesians 5:22–33), and Jesus sometimes refers to himself as the bridegroom (Matthew 9:15). But these references could be spiritualized and used also as support for the denial of earthly marriage in favor of a mystical union with God. Therefore Christian marriages—which point to God's grace and which are oriented toward ministry and a reflection of the good gift of sexuality—can bring balance to the issue.

—ISABEL ANDERS IN *AWAITING THE CHILD: AN ADVENT JOURNAL*

Most gracious God, we give you thanks for your tender love in sending Jesus Christ to come among us, to be born of a human mother, and to make the way of the cross to be the way of life. We thank you, also, for consecrating the union of man and woman in his Name. By the power of your Holy Spirit, pour out the abundance of your blessing upon this man and this woman. Defend them from every enemy. Lead them into all peace. Let their love for each other be a seal upon their hearts, a mantle about their shoulders, and a crown upon their foreheads. Bless them in their work and in their companionship; in their sleeping and in their waking; in their joys and in their sorrows; in their life and in their death. Finally, in your mercy, bring them to that table where your saints feast for ever in your heavenly home; through Jesus Christ our Lord, who with you and the Holy Spirit lives and reigns, one God, for ever and ever. Amen.

—PRAYER FOR MARRIAGE FROM *THE BOOK OF COMMON PRAYER*

Set me as a seal upon thine heart, as a seal upon thine arm: for love is strong as death…the flashes thereof are flashes of fire, a very flame of the Lord.

—SONG OF SOLOMON 8:6, *ENGLISH REVISED VERSION*

What greater thing is there for two human souls than to feel that they are joined for life—to strengthen each other in all labor, to rest on each other in all sorrow, to minister to each other in all pain, to be one with each other in silent, unspeakable memories at the moment of the last parting?

—GEORGE ELIOT IN *ADAM BEDE*

Lord, make us instruments of your peace.
Where there is hatred, let us sow love;
Where there is injury, pardon;
Where there is discord, union;
Where there is doubt, faith;
Where there is despair, hope;
Where there is darkness, light;
Where there is sadness, joy;
O Divine Master,
Grant that we may not so much seek
To be consoled as to console,
To be understood as to understand,
To be loved as to love.
For it is in giving that we receive;
It is in pardoning that we are pardoned;
And it is in dying that we are born to eternal life. Amen.

—SAINT FRANCIS OF ASSISI

Right now, my love
I would like to know
What you are thinking
What you are feeling.
This very moment
I know you are hurting deeply.
Your eyes always give you away.
But if for one reason
Or many reasons
You cannot tell me now
If words don't come easily
If somehow you are reluctant

To unlock the door of your heart
Please know I am with you
Just the same.
I will wait for you
With patience and understanding
Because I love you
With all there is of me.

—RUTH HARMS CALKIN IN *HOLD ME CLOSE*

Love one another, my dear children!
Seek rather what unites,
Not what may separate you
from one another.
As I take leave, or better still
As I say "till we meet again"
Let me remind you of the
most important things in life:
Our blessed Savior Jesus; His good news;
His holy Church: truth and kindness…

—POPE JOHN XXIII (1881–1963)

May the Lord who began His divine miracles at the wedding of
Cana of Galilee, bless you in your new life and bless your house
and transform things that create division into means of blessing,
and fill your hearts with spiritual love.

—FROM COPTIC WEDDING LITURGY

No, my darling
We are not going to have a perfect marriage.
No, we shall not experience
Only sweet and tender happiness.
We will not adore each other
Let alone like each other every moment of the day.
We will not cherish and obey
In sickness and health
For richer or poorer day after day after day.

Nor shall we have peace and contentment
Undivided attention
Acceptance and forgiveness
Without a single interruption
As long as we both shall live.

But yes, we will certainly make it!
It will be a beautiful adventure
As we experience our own limited resources
And God's limitless power.
He will teach us how to challenge
The difficulties of life.
And how to cherish the joys.
It will be worth all the variable mixture
For we shall learn it and do it with Him.

—RUTH HARMS CALKIN IN *HOLD ME CLOSE*

I exhort married persons to have that mutual love that is so earnestly enjoined by the Holy Spirit in Scripture. The first result of such love is the indissoluble union of your hearts. This spiritual union of the heart, with its affections and love, is stronger than that of mere bodily union.

—SAINT FRANCIS DE SALES (1567–1622)

Counting years is something children do—
But love reminds us every year
on our wedding anniversary
that adding up our years together
gives us strength
renews our hope
makes us laugh
and
counteracts the usual effect
of knowing we are growing older.

Instead, it reminds us that:
A life can be measured in richness, not length.
That each day, each moment is a gift.
That I choose you (and you me)
for all that we have known
and experienced together—
and for all that lies ahead—
as God gives us breath and life…
because you are you!

—ISABEL ANDERS

[Alternate lines or stanzas can be read aloud by the partners.]

A wedding is for a day
A marriage for a life—as God grants us enduring grace
In which to love and thrive.

You are our dwelling-place, O Lord.
Yet for this earthly journey
You have graciously offered us love's presence
Embodied in one another:
To be each other's nearest neighbor
To be companioned through the inevitable straits of life
To hear a voice beside us in the dark
And know the healing touch of a loving embrace.

We commit ourselves anew
To the truth of our wedding vows: that You alone
Can make two become one.

Remind us daily of the gift
That comes with every breath we take:
That unless God builds a house,
They labor in vain to construct one.

Let wisdom build its house in us
And may our decisions and our actions
Fortify its walls and add to its splendor
Now, and in all the years ahead
As you continue to bless our marriage and our love.
Amen.

—ISABEL ANDERS

Might common prayer and a sense of humility be the same thing, moving at different speeds…a sense of humility, just common prayer, dancing?

—LANE DENSON III

SPOUSES' PRAYER FOR EACH OTHER:

Dear God,
grant that I and my spouse may have a true
and understanding love for each other.
Grant that we may both
be filled with faith and trust.
Give us the grace to live
with each other in peace and harmony.
May we always bear with each other's weaknesses
and grow from each other's strengths.
Help us to forgive each other's failings
and grant us patience, kindness, cheerfulness,
and the spirit of placing the well-being
of each other ahead of self.

May the love that brought us together
grow and mature with each passing year.
Bring us both ever closer to You
through our love for each other.
Let our love grow to perfection.

—AUTHOR UNKNOWN

Questions for Further Reflection

1. Remember what your vow to "take" each other before God meant to you on your wedding day. What does it mean to you today?

2. How has the paradox of *two becoming one* both baffled and surprised you in the working out of your relationship through the years? What insights would you offer to a couple just entering the mystery of the marriage union?

3. Tell each other in plain words what praying together means to you. How is the practice of *praying* together connected to *playing* and *working* together?

4. What prayer disciplines do you wish to adopt in the days ahead, and how will you go about this? Consider these points:

    -   being there
    -   being open
    -   considering each other
    -   sensing God's presence
    -   taking God with you in whatever follows from these moments.

Loving in
All Weathers

"*For better
or for worse*"

How can we ever adequately describe the happiness of that marriage which the Church arranges, the Sacrifice strengthens, upon which the blessing sets a seal, at which angels are present as witnesses, and to which the Father gives His consent?

—TERTULLIAN (C. 160–255)

At Cana, Christ confirmed what He instituted in Paradise.

—SAINT AUGUSTINE OF HIPPO (354–430)

If all seasons nourish souls, then the vow "for better or for worse" is a necessary component to a loving commitment that can withstand the inevitable storms of married life.

Perhaps not all of us will have the opportunity to exercise Christlike grace in a visible, tangible way. Or again, maybe we all *do* have such moments when the choice of *self* against the best good for our spouse—and therefore for us as a couple—is posed. And in the moment we will choose to go one way or the other.

To feel deeply and be caught by the sweep of grace that allows *me to love you* and *you to love me* even through *this*—whatever the test may be—is the embodiment of the second half of the phrase "for better or for worse." The particulars that unfold are almost *never* what we think they will be. We aren't agreeing to a specific clause in a contract that outlines all our indemnities so that we sign on the dotted line with a completely informed will, agreeing to *only this.*

Christian marriage makes no sense to a purely secular mind —perhaps to most of the world—in the postmodern chaos of getting yours and getting it now. *New York Times* columnist David Brooks wrote about how cell phones have influenced the current level of what used to be courtship ("Cellphones, Texts and Lovers," November 2, 2009). He describes a ranking system that seems more about obtaining a commodity than about establishing a healthy relationship.

Brooks mourns the loss of values that once guided such a crucial part of life as sexual relationships. People enjoyed a lifestyle that promoted emotional maturity, supported permanent commitments, and connected everyday wants to higher things. He credits the collective wisdom of the community with guiding couples in their commitment to each other.

It is within this community of values that still exists in the Church—of people who *do not* feel that unconditional love, fidelity, reciprocity, and trust are old-fashioned or can be discarded along with obsolete technology—*that vows are taken.* And it is this community that can help us keep our marriage vows, as best as is possible, for more than our own gain.

In his Second Letter to the Corinthians, Saint Paul says, "We look not at what can be seen but at what cannot be seen; for what can be seen is temporary, but what cannot be seen is eternal" (4:18).

What our vows are about is *love,* a power unseen by eyes but easily demonstrated in our day-to-day choices and actions toward each other. It is that simple and that profound. Love makes all the difference.

Thoughts, Prayers, and Blessings

From every human being there rises a light that reaches straight to heaven, and when two souls that are destined to be together find each other, the streams of light flow together and a single brighter light goes forth from that united being.

—BA'AL SHEM TOV (1698–1760)

The Church asks the bride and groom: "What guarantee will you give that you will love one another until death do you part?" If they say: "We give the pledge of our word," the Church will answer: "Words and pacts can be broken, as the history of our world too well proves." If they say: "We give the pledge of a ring," the Church will again answer: "Rings can be broken and lost, and with them the memory of a promise. Only when you stake your eternal salvation as a guarantee of your fidelity to represent the union of Christ and the Church, will the Church consent to unite you as man and wife." Their lives thus become bonded at the altar, sealed with the seal of the Cross, and signed with the Eucharist, which they both receive into their souls as a pledge of the unity in Spirit, which is the foundation of their unity in the flesh.

—ARCHBISHOP FULTON SHEEN IN *THREE TO GET MARRIED*

NOTE FROM AUTHOR:
This position may seem extreme to us in our admitted failures to live up to so great an image as Christ and the Church. Yet what comes through clearly and importantly here is that marriage offers its partners perhaps the most important and challenging opportunity of their lives, in its intimacy and exclusivity, to

grow into people with souls—whose actions toward the spouse, the nearest neighbor, are every day in some ways determining what we are becoming and toward which destination we proceed: heaven or hell.

I adjure you, O daughters of Jerusalem,
by the gazelles or the wild does:
do not stir up or awaken love until it is ready!

The voice of my beloved!
Look, he comes,
leaping upon the mountains, bounding over the hills.
My beloved is like a gazelle or a young stag.
Look, there he stands behind our wall,
gazing in at the windows, looking through the lattice.
My beloved speaks and says to me:
"Arise, my love, my fair one,
and come away;
for now the winter is past,
the rain is over and gone.
The flowers appear on the earth;
the time of singing has come,
and the voice of the turtle-dove
is heard in our land.
The fig tree puts forth its figs,
and the vines are in blossom;
they give forth fragrance.
Arise, my love, my fair one,
and come away.

O my dove, in the clefts of the rock,
in the covert of the cliff,
let me see your face,
let me hear your voice;
for your voice is sweet,
and your face is lovely.
Catch us the foxes,
the little foxes,
that ruin the vineyards—
for our vineyards are in blossom."

My beloved is mine and I am his;
he pastures his flock among the lilies.
Until the day breathes
and the shadows flee,
turn, my beloved, be like a gazelle
or a young stag on the cleft mountains.

—SONG OF SOLOMON 2:7–17

"I told you so!"
We both know, Lord, how annoying and irritating
this self-righteous little phrase can be,
and yet we use it so often.

In fact, there are times, Lord,
when it actually feels good
to be able to say it—
when it feels good
to be able to gloat over the fact
that I was right
and my partner was wrong.

Let us learn, Lord,
how to avoid responding to our loved ones
with such pettiness and spite.

Teach us how to be
not only more kind and tolerant
of each other's mistakes
but also more understanding
of each other's occasional
lack of judgment.

Let us always remember, Lord, that nobody,
including us,
ever goes through life
without making mistakes.

—RENEE BARTKOWSKI IN *PRAYERS FOR MARRIED COUPLES*

May God the Father bless us, may Christ take care of us, the
Holy Ghost enlighten us all the days of our life. The Lord be our
defender and keeper of body and soul, both now and for ever,
to the ages of ages.

—SAINT ETHELWOLD

Slow to suspect—quick to trust.
Slow to condemn—quick to justify.
Slow to offend—quick to defend.
Slow to expose—quick to shield.
Slow to reprimand—quick to appreciate.
Slow to demand—quick to serve.
Slow to provoke—quick to conciliate.
Slow to hinder—quick to help.
Slow to resent—quick to forgive.

—GILES AND MELVILLE HARCOURT IN *SHORT PRAYERS FOR THE LONG DAY*

Come live with me and be my love,
And we will all the pleasures prove
That valleys, groves, hills, and fields,
Woods, or steepy mountain yields.

And we will sit upon the rocks,
Seeing the shepherds feed their flocks,
By shallow rivers to whose falls
Melodious birds sing madrigals.

And I will make thee beds of roses
And a thousand fragrant posies,
A cap of flowers and a kirtle
Embroider'd all with leaves of myrtle.

A gown made of the finest wool,
Which from our pretty lambs we pull;
Fair lined slippers for the cold,
With buckles of the purest gold.

A belt of straw and ivy buds,
With coral clasps and amber studs:
And if these pleasures may thee move,
Come live with me and be my love.

The shepherd swains shall dance and sing
For thy delight each May morning:
If these delights thy mind may move,
Then live with me and be my love.

—CHRISTOPHER MARLOWE (1564–1593) IN
THE PASSIONATE SHEPHERD TO HIS LOVE

May God give you…
For every storm, a rainbow,
For every tear, a smile,
For every care, a promise,
And a blessing in each trial.
For every problem life sends,
A faithful friend to share,
For every sigh, a sweet song,
And an answer for each prayer.
Amen.

—TRADITIONAL IRISH PRAYER

Bless the Lord, O my soul,
and all that is within me,
bless his holy name.
Bless the Lord, O my soul,
and do not forget all his benefits—
who forgives all your iniquity,
who heals all your diseases,
who redeems your life from the Pit,
who crowns you with steadfast love and mercy,
who satisfies you with good as long as you live
so that your youth is renewed like the eagle's.

—PSALM 103:1–5

I arise today
Through the strength of heaven;
Light of the sun,
Splendor of fire,
Speed of lightning,
Swiftness of the wind,
Depth of the sea,
Stability of the earth,
Firmness of the rock.

I arise today
Through God's strength to pilot me;
God's might to uphold me,
God's wisdom to guide me,
God's eye to look before me,
God's ear to hear me,
God's word to speak for me,
God's hand to guard me,
God's way to lie before me,
God's shield to protect me,
God's hosts to save me
Afar and anear,
Alone or in a multitude.

Christ shield me today
Against wounding
Christ with me,
Christ before me,
Christ behind me,
Christ in me,
Christ beneath me,

Christ above me,

Christ on my right,

Christ on my left,

Christ when I lie down,

Christ when I sit down,

Christ in the heart of everyone who thinks of me,

Christ in the mouth of everyone who speaks of me,

Christ in the eye that sees me,

Christ in the ear that hears me.

I arise today

Through the mighty strength

Of the Lord of creation.

—FROM THE LORICA, OR ST. PATRICK'S BREASTPLATE

I add my breath to your breath

that our days may be long on the Earth,

that the days of our people may be long,

that we shall be as one person,

that we may finish our road together.

—PUEBLO SONG

Christ has adorned your souls with perennial riches, and He has enriched both of you with holy wedding gifts—hope, devotion, fidelity, peace, chastity.

—PAULINUS OF NOLA (C. 353–431)

Your task is not to seek for love, but merely to seek and find all the barriers within yourself that you have built against it.

—RUMI

Incandescence. I have seen it on my husband's face—as he spoke his vows to me once on a cloudless afternoon, and in his faithful, self-forgetting devotion to me on myriad occasions since.

In human faces and in earthly time, God makes known to us the riches of this mystery: Christ in us, the hope of glory. If the kingdom is here and now, then it is no wonder that some of its characteristics occasionally seep out—shine out—from the midst of our mundane, earthbound experience, reminding us of our true destiny.

—ISABEL ANDERS IN *SOUL MOMENTS: TIMES WHEN HEAVEN TOUCHES EARTH*

Marriage is an act of will that signifies and involves a mutual gift, which unites the spouses and binds them to their eventual souls, with whom they make up a sole family—a domestic church.

—POPE JOHN PAUL II

As we continue our journey together, I pray not for continual sunshine, but for mutual patience and loving endurance through the ever-changing weathers of life.

Let us be shelter to each other, a home in the midst of storm, a burning flame to shed light in the darkness.

Give us continued strength and grace to remember the sun when it is not shining, to believe in God's care and love when we cannot know outcomes, and to endure with each other through uncertainties and fears.

Let us be shelter to each other, a home in the midst of storm, a burning flame to shed light in the darkness.

Show us the way to go forward when the path ahead seems blocked or clouded with doubts and obstacles to our union. We ask for perseverance to forgive and to believe again.

Let us be shelter to each other, a home in the midst of storm, a burning flame to shed light in the darkness.

Through all the seasons of our life together, grant us growth in grace, maturity in love, the joyful blessings of physical union, and the ability to continue to pray together in one spirit.

Let us be shelter to each other, a home in the midst of storm, a burning flame to shed light in the darkness—for Jesus' own sake. Amen.

—ISABEL ANDERS

Questions for Further Reflection

1. What are the greatest impediments to a lifelong marriage of fidelity and trust? What choices can lessen outside influences that may threaten our core commitment to each other and the free exercise of forgiving love?

2. Describe some of the "weathers" marriage may take you through: storms, floods, winds, sunny days, and blizzards. What steps can you take in each symbolic season or siege of weather to withstand the changes and the challenges of "for better or for worse"?

3. What experiences of your marriage can you share regularly, what stories serve as reminders of your keeping your vows through these seasons and phases of decision-making? What can you both learn from times of failure to take each other's part? How did you repair the damage from those failures?

4. How can praying together provide the "ammunition" needed to strengthen your ongoing relationship? Blessed Teresa of Calcutta once recounted the following incident: "When I was crossing into Gaza, I was asked at the checkpost whether I was carrying any weapons. I replied, 'Oh, yes, my prayer books.'" How can mutual prayer be a potent "weapon" against separation and loss in marriage?

In Flesh
and Spirit

"To have
and to hold"

At the beginning God formed two creatures, Adam and Eve; that is, man and wife. He formed the woman from the man, from the rib of Adam. He bade them both to live in one body and one spirit.

—AMBROSE OF MILAN (C. 339–397)

How beautiful is the marriage of two Christians, two who are one in hope, one in desire, one in the way of life they follow, one in the religion they practice. They are, in very truth, two in one flesh; and where there is but one flesh there is also but one spirit. They pray together, they worship together, they fast together; instructing one another, strengthening one another.

—TERTULLIAN (C. 160–255)

Marriage is good for those who are afraid to sleep alone at night.

—SAINT JEROME (C. 340–420)

If we take matrimony at its lowest, we regard it as a sort of friendship recognized by the police.

—ROBERT LOUIS STEVENSON

Marital love is a reflection of how God loves. It is free, total, faithful and fruitful.

—CHRISTOPHER WEST IN *THEOLOGY OF THE BODY*

An anonymous Sufi master is quoted as saying, "If you put the world between you and God, the world becomes a spiritual obstacle; if you use the world to remember God, the world becomes your spiritual friend."

Somewhere between Saint Jerome's concession that marital love has a practical application and the scriptural principles that form the Church's ideal template for marriage lies (pun intended) the reality of the physical marital union. Yes, marriage is spiritual—but it is, simultaneously, a physical union blessed by God and endorsed by Jesus in his attendance at the wedding at Cana where he performed his first public miracle.

As a particular man and a particular woman, we bring together in the actuality and commitment of our vows an instance of paradox, of opposites, of the ideal meeting face-to-face with the fallen realities of earthly humanness.

Marriage may begin in a glow of optimism and even exultation. But the realities of living together soon catch up with even the most passionate couple.

Christian marriage provides us with perhaps the most intense and demanding opportunity to live both as individuals and as a unit—a family—sometimes referred to as a "little church."

Just as governments and institutions have rites and ceremonies that strengthen unity and allow members to affirm their connection and their mutual purpose, so prayers designed for married couples can offer a way of reminder and recommitment as they are worked into the fabric of daily life together.

Having our homes blessed room by room is a wonderful way to set a precedent for inviting God into the space and everyday functions of our house and its occupants, including our life of intimacy.

As human creatures, we are a mysterious blend of flesh and spirit. How we live into this reality is as personal as our handprint. But because others have gone before us into this mystery, we also have help in learning to live on more than one level.

In his book *Splendor in the Ordinary* (Tyndale House, 1976), Thomas Howard takes readers on a tour through the many rooms of a home in which the rites of love are carried out—eating, making love, sleeping, sometimes even being born and dying. God created the physical elements as well as the spiritual, reminding us of the primary sacraments of baptism and Eucharist—sacraments Howard describes as "unabashedly physical."

Howard speaks of the bedroom as the room in which we are most likely to experience the "to have and to hold" of the wedding vow. We know Adam and Eve had physical relations. Howard finds it somewhat ironic that our most profound knowledge as intellectual and spiritual beings comes from the ordinary business of "skin on skin."

The author of the Letter to the Hebrews wrote, "Let marriage be held in honor by all, and let the marriage bed be kept undefiled" (13:4). This straightforward acknowledgment both defines and validates the cornerstone of *fidelity in physical union* on which Christian marriage is built.

All of this may seem "quaint" and antiquated to those who have not been shaped by the Church's teaching and therefore have not been "held back" by the restraints of marriage vows. But no one wants to be cheated on or made a fool of. Even our current culture—which largely denies the importance of these values—tends to "blame" and make a bad example of those who publicly defy its unacknowledged rules.

As believers, we affirm that Christian marriage initiates us to higher levels of God's purposes for humanity. The order and spiritual meaning inherent in the Christian view of marriage is something that today is longed for and often goes unperceived—as selfishness runs rampant. As couples choose, by grace, to live by its light, they can become the lights to the world that Jesus calls them to be.

Thoughts, Prayers, and Blessings

All that exists is gained in two steps: by lifting up the foot from self-interest and setting it down on the commandments of God.

—AN ANCIENT PROVERB

Be transformed by the renewing of your minds.

—ROMANS 12:2

We are to practice virtue, not possess it.

—MEISTER ECKHART

Learn now to die to the world, so shalt thou begin to live with Christ.

—THOMAS À KEMPIS IN *THE IMITATION OF CHRIST*

Since the Second Vatican Council, a liturgical renewal has taken root and blossomed in the Catholic Church. The heart of this renewal is prayer. Prayer happens not only in the Sunday liturgy but also in our households—the "little churches" of the faithful.

As an act of love, prayer is a courageous act. It is a risk we take. It is a life-and-death risk, believing in the promises of the gospel, that God's love is indeed operative in the world. In prayer we have the courage, perhaps even the presumption and the arrogance or the audacity to claim that God's love can be operative in the very specific situations of human need that we encounter.

—JOHN E. BIERSDORF IN *HEALING OF PURPOSE*

Beloved, we are God's children now; what we will be has not yet been revealed. What we do know is this: when he is revealed, we will be like him, for we will see him as he is.

—1 JOHN 3:2

Lord Jesus, grant that I and my spouse may have a true and understanding love for each other. Grant that we may both be filled with faith and trust. Give us the grace to live with each other in peace and harmony. May we always bear with one another's weaknesses and grow from each other's strengths. Help us to forgive one another's failings and grant us patience, kindness, cheerfulness and the spirit of placing the well-being of one another ahead of self.

May the love that brought us together grow and mature with each passing year. Bring us both ever closer to You through our love for each other. Let our love grow to perfection. Amen.

—FROM THE BOOK OF BLESSINGS BY THE
CONGREGATION FOR DIVINE WORSHIP

All the wealth in the world cannot be compared with the happiness of living together happily united.

—BLESSED MARGARET D'YOUVILLE

What is it men in women do require?
The lineaments of gratified desire.
What is it women do in men require?
The lineaments of gratified desire.

—WILLIAM BLAKE (1757–1827)

O Lord, inflame these lovers with the fire of love. In the morning of all their days, may they awake unto joy!

I will give my love an apple without e'er a core
I will give my love a house without e'er a door,
I will give my love a palace wherein she may be,
But she may unlock it without any key.

My head is the apple without e'er a core,
My mind is the house without e'er a door.
My heart is the palace wherein she may be
And she may unlock it without e'er a key.

Lord God, Creator of the universe, Father of us all, we have gathered here around this dinner table to celebrate the love and commitment that have united N. and N. in a wonderful bond of marriage. Bless, Father, this food that we are about to receive with grateful hearts as a sign of your continuous bounty and providence. May your generous blessing descend also upon these spouses, their families and friends present here at this joyful banquet. We make this prayer in the name of Jesus our Lord and Savior, who lives and reigns with You and the Holy Spirit, one God for ever and ever. Amen.

O Great Spirit, whose breath gives life to the world,
and whose voice is heard in the soft breeze:
We need your strength and wisdom.

Cause us to walk in beauty.
Give us eyes ever to behold the red and purple sunset.
Make us wise so that we may understand
what you have taught us.

Help us learn the lessons you have hidden in every leaf and rock.
Make us always ready to come to you
with clean hands and steady eyes,
so when life fades, like the fading sunset,
our spirits may come to you without shame.

—NATIVE AMERICAN PRAYER

Bless *N.* and *N.* on the road of life together. May they respect each other's likes and dislikes, opinions and beliefs, hopes and dreams, troubles and fears, even though they may not always understand each other.

May they rest in the knowledge that no matter what happens, by holding on to each other things will work out for the best.

Most of all, dear God, help them to keep the torch of love burning with the fire that they now share in their hearts. Amen.

—WEDDING PRAYER, ADAPTED

The great danger for family life, in the midst of any society whose idols are pleasure, comfort and independence, lies in the fact that people close their hearts and become selfish.

—POPE JOHN PAUL II

I take you again this day "to have and to hold."

Teach us, Lord, how to enjoy and accompany and give ourselves to each other without possession.

As we cherish the blessings of bodies and spirits, finding unity at times and struggling to understand each other at times, give us the grace to blend these experiences into a whole we can embrace as committed marriage.

Help us learn to laugh together, to cry when needed, to pick ourselves and each other up from where we may have fallen— and to go forward together.

Bless our bodies and our minds, our hearts and our spirits, as we offer them to you today without reservation, knowing that you have made us in love and have taught us to love one another. *Therefore we pray together:* Our Father…

—ISABEL ANDERS

I think the world today is upside down. Everybody seems to be in such a terrible rush, anxious for greater development and greater riches and so on. There is much suffering because there is so very little love in homes and in family life. We have no time for our children, we have no time for each other; there is no time to enjoy each other. In the home begins the disruption of the peace of the world.

—BLESSED TERESA OF CALCUTTA

P: Pastor; *C:* Congregation

P: Let love be genuine and live in harmony;
hate what is evil, hold fast to what is good.
Outdo one another in showing honor;
be humble and never conceited.

C: Love is stronger than death
and jealousy is cruel as the grave.
Floods cannot drown love
and wealth cannot buy it.

P: Put love above all else;
let Christ's peace rule your hearts.
Always be forgiving,
as Christ has forgiven you.

C: Love is not jealous or boastful,
arrogant, rude or stubborn,
irritable, resentful or possessive.
Love is patient and kind.

P: Do not love in word or speech only;
love also in deed and truth.
Receive each other in sincerity,
find mercy and grow old together.

C: Love rejoices in the right;
it bears, believes, hopes and endures all things,
for love is faithful and endless.

P: When the Lord builds the house,
the labor is never in vain.

C: Happy are those who take refuge in God;
those who serve the Lord are redeemed.

P: This is my commandment,
that you love one another as I have loved you.

C: And two shall become one in love,
for we are members of Christ's body.

—AUTHOR UNKNOWN

It takes guts to stay married....There will be many crises between the wedding day and the golden anniversary, and the people who make It are heroes.

—HOWARD WHITMAN

Love is a fire that can never be put out. It is the vital source of the flames of true faith enlightening the hearts of real believers. Love of God sets them on fire with a faith they could never enjoy if they did not already love him in their hearts.

—HILDEGARD OF BINGEN (1098–1179)

Questions for Further Reflection

1. What does the physical nature of the sacraments—the acts we offer to God in our worship—teach us about the sacramental nature of our life together?

2. What have we learned through the years of living together that we did not perceive or imagine when we first took our vow "to have and to hold"? What would we advise young couples to consider about their physical loyalty as they make their commitment to build a Christian home together?

3. What does it mean to "die to the world," and how can we continue to live as human beings if we submit to such an ideal?

4. What do the physical acts and nature of the marriage union teach us about the love of Christ for the Church in both practical and spiritual terms? How do the nature of man and the nature of woman enhance for us the reciprocity of this image and its meaning for us as a couple?

Through Sun
and Shadow

"In good times
and in bad"

Every tomorrow has two handles. We can take hold of it with the handle of anxiety or the handle of faith.
—HENRY WARD BEECHER

We know that all things work together for good for those who love God, who are called according to his purpose.
—ROMANS 8:28

Our trials are suited to our need as the glove to the hand of the wearer.
—SAINT ALPHONSUS LIGUORI

In a *Peanuts* cartoon, Charlie Brown asks Lucy why life is so hard and full of adversity. She replies that adversity is good for us because it builds character. Charlie Brown then wants to know why we need character, to which Lucy answers, *to cope with adversity.*

Sometimes we may feel it is not the outer circumstances we are battling but the circumstances of *living with each other* and our differences.

A story is told of an expert in diamonds who happened to be seated on an airplane beside a woman with a huge diamond on her finger. The man introduced himself and said, "I couldn't help but notice your beautiful diamond. I am an expert in precious stones. Please tell me about that stone."

The woman replied, "That is the famous Klopman diamond,

one of the largest in the world. But there is a strange curse that comes with it." Now the man was really interested. He asked, "What is the curse?" As he waited with bated breath, she replied, "It's Mr. Klopman."

In one episode of a long-running TV series, the spouses confronted each other about why their marriage wasn't working. She listed a number of things for which she had forgiven him, but then noted his most recent transgression and said, "And for that, I can't forgive you." He countered by saying, "I am your husband and you didn't even give me the benefit of the doubt before deciding I was guilty. For that, *I can't forgive you*."

It was practically a parody of what Christian marriage should be about. One thing it is *not* about is focusing on the latest grievance or setting up one criterion for sticking together or for giving up. That position fails to consider that *this is what marriage is*—the working out of our differences in the context of the love that holds us "in good times and in bad."

A master of a school of wisdom grew tired of his assistant's complaints and so sent him out one morning to obtain some salt. When the assistant returned, the master told the dour young man to place a handful of salt in a glass of water and then drink it.

"How does it taste?" the master asked.

"It is bitter," complained the young man, sputtering as he spat out a mouthful.

The wise master simply laughed and asked the young man to take the same amount of salt and pour it into the lake. They walked together silently to the nearby water's edge. Once the apprentice had put his handful of salt into the water, the old man instructed him, "Now take a drink from the lake."

As water dripped from the young man's beard, his master asked him again, "How does it taste?"

"Just right," admitted the assistant.

"Can you taste any salt?" asked the master.

"None," admitted the young man.

This serious young man reminded the master of himself at an earlier stage of his training. He told him compassionately: "You must realize that the sorrow in life is simply *salt*, by itself bitter. The amount of distress you will experience in life may be constant. But the amount of its *bitterness* that you taste depends on the container in which you put the sorrow. So when you are hurting, all you can do is to enlarge your 'container.' You must no longer be a glass. You must become a lake."

The line of the marriage vow that compels two people to remain *one* "in good times and in bad" is a call to "become a lake"—to seek to embrace the larger spiritual context in which your relationship rests; to allow the divine sun to overcome momentary shadow—in this moment and *as a habit* that can carry you through to the next resting place, where it may all seem worth it after all.

"God," the elder in a traditional wisdom parable said, "is closer to sinners than to saints."

"But how can that be?" the eager disciple asked.

The elder explained: "God in heaven holds each person by a string. When we sin, we cut the string. Then God ties it up again, making a knot—bringing the sinner a little closer. Again and again sins cut the string—and with each knot God keeps drawing the string closer and closer. That is how sinners become nearer to God."

Thoughts, Prayers, and Blessings

The fruit of the Spirit is love, joy, peace, patience, kindness, generosity, faithfulness.

—GALATIANS 5:22

When, good Lord, will you manifest yourself to us in bright sunshine? Yes, we are slow to understand and slow to see. But we are quick to believe; and we believe that if you chose to reveal yourself to us, you could do so this very day.

Our Lord, nourish with the riches of Your grace these Your servants who are united together, and make them joyful with Your gift. Satisfy them with the perfection of Your divine commandments, that they may sing praises unto You with exceeding joy, and be happy before You.

—SYRIAN WEDDING LITURGY

My dearest Jesus, I have told all my sins to the best of my ability. I have sincerely tried to make a good confession and I know that You have forgiven me. Thank You, dear Jesus! Your Divine Heart is full of love and mercy for sinners. I love You, dear Jesus; You are so good to me. My loving Savior, I shall try to keep from sin and to love more each day. Dearest Mother Mary, pray for me and help me to keep all my promises. Protect me and do not let me fall back into sin. Dear God, help me to lead a good life. Without Your grace I can do nothing. Amen.

—PRAYER AFTER CONFESSION, TRADITIONAL

Dr. Rollo R. May, in his work *The Art of Counseling* (Nashville, Abingdon, 1978) presented what he calls "the psychology of temptation." His first point is that this psychology is not well understood by religious people, people who are long on exhortation and short on the nuances of the situation. This lopsidedness leads to the "fish in the net" syndrome. That is, like fish caught in a net, the more people fight to get free of the temptation they resist, the more enmeshed in the "net" they become. Their last state is worse than the first.

White-knuckling their way into "self-mastery," they get steamrolled by the forces of the unconscious, which mock such perfectionism. The "dark side" eventually erupts, and the ensuing volcano of unmanageability leads to intense feelings of guilt and a debilitating sense of worthlessness.

May contends that most temptations are not overcome by a direct "frontal" attack. In fact, especially in matters of desire, the more the "thou shalt not" is emphasized, the more vivid the desire gets, and the stronger the temptation becomes.

The best way to defuse the power of temptation, May insists, is to remove the image from the center of one's attention—which is precisely what Jesus does with Satan. He does not deny or repress the temptations; rather, Jesus lifts them to a higher plane than "self-conquest." He yields them to God.

He sees them in light of God's holy love, and within the context of God's call on his life—a messiahship of servant leadership. Jesus doesn't fight the satanic temptations by dwelling on them; he submits them to the power and grace of God. It is a power revealed in Scripture, and made operative through the Holy Spirit.

—H. KING OEHMIG IN *SYNTHESIS*

Dear Lord, we have an important decision to make
and neither of us seems to be able to determine
what the right decision should be.

We have taken the time to examine all of the options
and their consequences,
and we still feel terribly confused and uncertain.

O Lord, don't let us go on floundering in this way.

You promised that you would help us
if only we would ask.

You promised that you would always
instruct us and direct us
in the way we should go.

We believe in your promises, dear Lord,
and we believe in your wisdom.

So guide us and show us the way,
give us the strength,
the confidence,
and the wisdom we need
not only to make the right decisions,
but also to have the ability
to accept the decisions that are right.

—RENEE BARTKOWSKI IN *PRAYERS FOR MARRIED COUPLES*

Be with us, Lord, tonight. Stay to accompany and give shelter to us while we sleep; to draw down mercy and grace upon the world. Stay with us to guard the innocent, to sustain the tempted, to raise the fallen, to curb the power of the evil one, to prevent sin. Stay with us to comfort the sorrowing. Stay, above all, with the suffering and dying to grant them contrition, to receive into the arms of Your mercy the thousands that this night must face their end. Secure them against the perils that beset them. Grant us a quiet night and a perfect end. Be our merciful Shepherd to the last, that without fear we may appear before You at the last day.

—EVENING PRAYER, TRADITIONAL

"How does marriage free as well as bind lovers?" the Daughter asked wonderingly.

"To me, freedom is to know that my love is lovingly returned," her Mother said simply.

—ISABEL ANDERS IN
BECOMING FLAME: UNCOMMON MOTHER-DAUGHTER WISDOM

Let no one ever come to you without leaving better and happier.

—BLESSED TERESA OF CALCUTTA

I take you through sun and rain
Whatever the skies above us will provide
In light and in shadow, to be the one who walks beside me.
To be the heart that touches mine
The hand that reaches to bridge any gulf
The resolute will that searches, with my own,
to find a path to lead us forward together.
Lord God, bless our loving intent to be
Double-souled on this earthly journey.
Teach us both our limitations,
and yet continue to grant us joys beyond measure,
You who blessed the Wedding of Cana with your presence and,
who created, out of scarcity,
an abundance of wine, overflowing.

Let us toil as well as feast together
For all our days
Forgiving each other, showing each other how
Two may be one in the mystery of union
As you, Father, Son, and Spirit
Dwell in perfect unity both here and above.

For Jesus' sake,
Amen.

—ISABEL ANDERS

PRAYER OF A MILITARY WIFE:

Dear God, I am proud to be wed to one who defends freedom and peace. My challenges are many and I pray for Your love and guidance to meet them. Special to me are the symbols representing my religion, country, community, and home. I pray for the wisdom and grace to be true to their meanings. You are the symbol of my religious beliefs and the source of my strength. Because my life is full of change, I cherish the solid and constant spiritual foundation that You provide. Help me, Lord, to be an example of Your teachings. My national flag represents freedom. Let me never forget, nor take for granted, the hope it shows to the world. Bless those who have made sacrifices for freedom. Please grant us Your continued blessings, increased strength, and infinite guidance as we live to Your honor and glory. Amen.

—AUTHOR UNKNOWN

Spouse: I choose you today to be my spouse, not in perfection but in acceptance, forgiveness, and love.

Response: I choose you today to be my spouse, not in perfection but in acceptance, forgiveness, and love.

Spouse: As we experience the light and blessing, the shadows and testings, we offer our lives to Christ for healing and continuance, and the grace, faithfully, to keep our vows for all our days.

Response: Grant us strength and hope, perseverance and joy on this path we walk together in your name.

Amen.

—ISABEL ANDERS

...when we find ourselves
In the place just right
It will be in the valley
Of love and delight.

—FROM SHAKER HYMN "SIMPLE GIFTS"

Grant me grace, O merciful God, to desire ardently all that is
pleasing to you, to examine it prudently, to acknowledge it
truthfully, and to accomplish it perfectly for the praise and glory
of your name. Amen.

—SAINT THOMAS AQUINAS

ODE TO A CAPABLE WIFE:
A capable wife who can find?
She is far more precious than jewels.
The heart of her husband trusts in her,
and he will have no lack of gain.
She does him good, and not harm,
all the days of her life.
She seeks wool and flax,
and works with willing hands.
She is like the ships of the merchant,
she brings her food from far away.
She rises while it is still night
and provides food for her household
and tasks for her servant-girls.
She considers a field and buys it;
with the fruit of her hands she plants a vineyard.
She girds herself with strength,
and makes her arms strong.

She perceives that her merchandise is profitable.
Her lamp does not go out at night.
She puts her hands to the distaff,
and her hands hold the spindle.
She opens her hand to the poor,
and reaches out her hands to the needy.
She is not afraid for her household when it snows,
for all her household are clothed in crimson.
She makes herself coverings;
her clothing is fine linen and purple.
Her husband is known in the city gates,
taking his seat among the elders of the land.
She makes linen garments and sells them;
she supplies the merchant with sashes.
Strength and dignity are her clothing,
and she laughs at the time to come.
She opens her mouth with wisdom,
and the teaching of kindness is on her tongue.
She looks well to the ways of her household,
and does not eat the bread of idleness.
Her children rise up and call her happy;
her husband too, and he praises her:
"Many women have done excellently,
but you surpass them all."
Charm is deceitful, and beauty is vain,
but a woman who fears the Lord is to be praised.
Give her a share in the fruit of her hands,
and let her works praise her in the city gates.

—PROVERBS 31

Blessed are you, Holy One of the Earth,
who creates the fruit of the vine.
Blessed are you, Holy One of the Universe.
You created all things for your glory.
Blessed are you, Holy One of the World.
Through you mankind lives.
Blessed are you, Holy One of the World.
You made man and woman in your image, after your likeness,
that they might perpetuate life....
Blessed are you, Holy One of All Nature,
who makes Zion rejoice with her children....
Blessed are you, Holy One of the Cosmos,
who makes the bridegroom and bride to rejoice.
Blessed are you, Holy One of All, who created joy and gladness,
bride and bridegroom, mirth and song, pleasure and delight,
love, fellowship, peace and friendship....

—TRADITIONAL HEBREW "SEVEN BLESSINGS"

If you think you are standing, watch out that you do not fall. No
testing has overtaken you that is not common to everyone. God
is faithful, and he will not let you be tested beyond your strength,
but with the testing he will also provide the way out so that you
may be able to endure it.…"All things are lawful," but not all things
are beneficial.…"All things are lawful," but not all things build up.
Do not seek your own advantage, but that of the other.

—1 CORINTHIANS 10:12–13, 23–24

Lord of all pots and pans and things;
since I've no time to be
a saint by doing lovely things or
watching late with Thee,
or dreaming in the dawnlight
or storming heaven's gates,
make me a saint by getting meals,
and washing up the plates.

Altho' I must have Martha's hands,
I have a Mary mind:
And when I black the boots and shoes,
Thy sandals, Lord, I find.
I think of how they trod the earth,
each time I scrub the floor;
Accept this meditation, Lord,
I haven't time for more.

Warm all the kitchen with Thy love,
and light it with Thy peace;
Forgive me all my worrying,
and make all grumbling cease.
Thou who didst love to give men food,
in room or by the sea,
Accept this service that I do—
I do it unto Thee.

—GILES AND MELVILLE HARCOURT IN
SHORT PRAYERS FOR THE LONG DAY

With three things I am delighted, for they are pleasing to the Lord and to men: Harmony among brethren, friendship among neighbors, and the mutual love of husband and wife.

—SIRACH 25:1, *NEW AMERICAN BIBLE*

For the faults of married people continually spur up each of them, hour by hour, to do better and to meet and love upon a higher ground.

—ROBERT LOUIS STEVENSON IN *VIRGINIBUS PUERISQUE*

Ten thousand things bright
Ten thousand miles, no dust
Water and sky one color
Houses shining along your road.

—CHINESE BLESSING

God continually showers the fullness of his grace on every being in the universe, but we consent to receive it to a greater or lesser extent. In purely spiritual matters, God grants all desires. Those who have less have asked for less.

—SIMONE WEIL IN *LETTER TO A PRIEST*

They feast on the abundance of your house, and you give them drink from the river of your delights.

—PSALM 36:8

Questions for Further Reflection

1. Think of a time when you might have been tempted to give up on your loved one. What brought you back to the larger reality of the blessing and challenge of your life together?

2. What is forgiveness, and what part does it play in long-term marriage between committed partners? How do the lessons of patience and forgiveness in marriage include implications for the treatment of people beyond the relationship?

3. How does our connectedness to other people in the world affect our sense of unity in marriage? Do we sometimes blame our spouse when other people and circumstances really are the cause of our distress? How can we work on this?

4. What spiritual principles and specific Bible passages enable us to hold each other in security and patience through good times and bad? What practices and disciplines can we undertake together to incorporate these truths into our day-to-day lives?

In Changing
Fortunes

"For richer
and for poorer"

O God, who transformed water into wine by Your divine power, bless Your two servants and purify them with Your love for mankind.

— COPTIC WEDDING LITURGY

An elderly woman approached British poet Samuel Taylor Coleridge after a lecture in the early 1800s and said, "Mr. Coleridge, I've accepted the universe!" Coleridge peered over the top of his glasses and said, "My God, madam, you'd better!"

— AUTHOR UNKNOWN

In the play *Fiddler on the Roof,* Tevye, a poor Jewish milkman, living in early twentieth-century Russia with five daughters and a wife, dreams of the material comforts wealth would bring him as he wistfully sings "If I Were a Rich Man." He contemplates owning a huge house filled with possessions, including interesting features such as a third staircase that leads nowhere and is just there to impress.

Of course, luxuries such as servants would make his wife's life easier, and having enough clothes and food would never again be a problem. The social status he would realize after being transformed into a wealthy man is no small factor to him either.

He also takes into consideration his spiritual side—the fact that he would have more time to attend synagogue and pray.

Surely God would take that into account in deciding to turn him into a wealthy man!

Times of wealth and of poverty—both possible arcs of experience that can occur during a marriage of any duration—are surely factors in maintaining unity, balance, hope, and a sense of humor along the way. Perhaps we feel with Tevye that even *God* might benefit by blessing us with more money in this life so that we could become better partners and disciples in practical ways.

The wisdom of Scripture offers insights that may remind us of Tevye's thoughts as we seek to take them to a deeper level that fits our lives as we live them now.

Ecclesiastes warns, "The lover of money will not be satisfied with money; nor the lover of wealth, with gain. This also is vanity" (5:10).

We need to remember that *we can't take credit* one way or the other, even if we feel our wealth or fortune is self-made. Jeremiah warns, "Thus says the Lord: Do not let the wise boast in their wisdom, do not let the mighty boast in their might, do not let the wealthy boast in their wealth" (9:23).

Paradoxically, if we are *not* well off and think we are therefore intrinsically wiser or better people, or if we *do* have money and congratulate ourselves on it, both stances have pitfalls when it comes to the Christian life.

It is difficult to get a handle on this issue of "for richer and for poorer," one aspect of the wedding vow that requires faith in what the future will bring. Some families find that in times of hardship or loss, they actually draw closer together, closer to God, and find more satisfaction in the small pleasures of life than when they are surrounded by plenty.

Of course, we do need money to survive as individuals and as a family, and money itself is not evil. As my husband often says when I hand him some bills from a bank cash withdrawal, "They won't clash with anything I'm wearing."

There are many ways to consider the importance of money in the context of a committed marriage. Most men and women today have jobs as well as family responsibilities.

Bestselling author James Patterson urges working people to think of life as a sort of game in which we juggle five balls labeled Work, Family, Health, Friends, and Integrity.

The ball for Work is like a rubber ball that will bounce back when dropped, he explains. The rest of the balls are made of glass and may be damaged or even shattered when dropped.

How we treat each other in times of poverty and wealth has important implications for our future with God and our ongoing unity with our marriage partner.

No one can serve two masters; for a slave will either hate the one and love the other, or be devoted to the one and despise the other. You cannot serve God and wealth.

—MATTHEW 6:24

How hard it will be for those who have wealth to enter the kingdom of God!

—MARK 10:23

It is easier for a camel to go through the eye of a needle than for someone who is rich to enter the kingdom of God.

—LUKE 18:25

Gracious God, Source of all life, Author of all that is true and good: give us the wind of your Holy Spirit that we may venture beyond the safe confines of an easy faith, and step out bravely from false security to carry the Gospel of Jesus Christ to a perishing world. All this we ask in the unity of the Godhead and in the power of your Holy Name. Amen.

—*UNDERSTANDING THE SUNDAY SCRIPTURES, YEAR B*

Never marry for money. Ye'll borrow it cheaper.

—SCOTTISH PROVERB

PRAYER FOR GENEROSITY:

Teach us, good Lord, to serve Thee as Thou deservest:
To give and not to count the cost;
To fight and not to heed the wounds;
To toil and not to seek for rest;
To labor and not to ask for any reward
Save that of knowing that we do Thy will.

—SAINT IGNATIUS OF LOYOLA (C. 1491–1556)

Our Father, which in heaven art,
Lord, Hallowed be thy Name.
Thy Kingdom come, thy will be done
In earth, even as the same
In heaven is. Give us, Lord,
Our daily bread this day.
As we forgive our debtors,
So forgive our debts, we pray.
Into temptation lead us not,
From evil keep us free:
For kingdom, power and glory is
Thine to eternity.

—STERNHOLD AND HOPKINS, *METRICAL PSALMS,* 1767

Saint Paul said that "the love of money"—not money itself—"is
the root of all kinds of evil."

—1 TIMOTHY 6:10

May love and laughter light your days,
and warm your heart and home.
May good and faithful friends be yours,
wherever you may roam.
May peace and plenty bless your world
with joy that long endures.
May all life's passing seasons
bring the best to you and yours!

—Ancient Irish blessing

Marriage halves our griefs, doubles our joys, and quadruples our expenses.

—English proverb

Bringing a service mentality to marriage is truly countercultural. It flies in the face of what our society has to say about marriage. Yet in viewing marriage as a form of "servanthood," serving each other, our family, and our world in the name of Jesus Christ, we have found a special kind of joy and fulfillment that can be understood only by doing it.

—William E. Rabior and Susan C. Rabior in
9 Ways to Nurture Your Marriage

May God be with you and bless you.
May you see your children's children.
May you be poor in misfortune,
rich in blessings.
May you know nothing but happiness
from this day forward.

—Irish blessing

We always try to be level-headed and thrifty
when it comes to managing our money.

But there are times, Lord, when our budget-balancing
leaves us whirling helplessly on that
"borrowing from Peter to pay Paul" merry-go-round.

There are times
when all the pennies we pinch
get the best of us and make us totally incapable
of agreeing on how to manage our money.

O Lord, don't ever let our financial problems
drive a wedge into our relationship.

Teach us how to resolve our difficulties
without arguments and disagreements.

Let us learn how to use good judgment
in trying to balance our budget
and to avoid being tempted to live beyond our means.

Endow each of us, Lord,
with both a sense of value and a sense of thrift
that will enable us to manage our money
not only more wisely and efficiently
but also more agreeably.

—RENEE BARTKOWSKI IN *PRAYERS FOR MARRIED COUPLES*

When the Lord restored the fortunes of Zion,
we were like those who dream.
Then our mouth was filled with laughter,
and our tongue with shouts of joy;
then it was said among the nations,
"The Lord has done great things for them."
The Lord has done great things for us,
and we rejoiced.
Restore our fortunes, O Lord,
like the watercourses in the Negeb.
May those who sow in tears
reap with shouts of joy.
Those who go out weeping,
bearing the seed for sowing,
shall come home with shouts of joy,
carrying their sheaves.

—PSALM 126

Give us, Lord, a humble, quiet, peaceable, patient, tender, and charitable mind, and in all our thoughts, words, and deeds a taste of the Holy Spirit. Give us, Lord, a lively faith, a firm hope, a fervent charity, and love of you. Take from us a lukewarmness in meditation, dullness in prayer. Give us fervor and delight in thinking of you and your grace, your tender compassion toward us. The things we pray for, good Lord, give us grace to labor for: through Jesus Christ our Lord.

—SAINT THOMAS MORE

I will hear what the Lord has to say to me:
for he will speak peace to his people,
and to his saints, and to those
who are converted in the heart.

Surely, his salvation is near
to those who fear him:
that glory may dwell in our land.

Mercy and truth have met each other:
justice and peace have kissed.
Truth has sprung out of the earth,
and justice has looked down from heaven.

For the Lord will bestow goodness,
and our earth shall yield her fruit.

—FROM PSALM 85, ADAPTED

Entreat me not to leave thee,
Or to return from following after thee:
For whither thou goest, I will go,
And where thou lodgest, I will lodge.
Thy people shall be my people,
And thy God my God:
Where thou diest, will I die,
And there will I be buried:
The Lord do so to me, and more also,
If ought but death part thee and me.

—RUTH 1:16–17, *KING JAMES VERSION*

A man who had been fabulously rich and powerful in his life on earth woke up and found himself in a small, dark room. He felt it had to be some mistake. Then he remembered the operation, the pain, the floating away from the table…the silence and the blackness.

He shook himself awake. Surely, no matter where he had ended up in the afterlife, there would be some provision! He rang a small bell that lay by his side. Sure enough, a steward came to his door, bearing a covered platter. His stomach growled as he greedily lifted the top. There, on a plain, rough board, lay one dirty pastry, smashed on one side and sprinkled with soot.

"Ugh!" he muttered. "Where's my meal? Is this some kind of joke?"

The steward merely nodded and left silently.

Sighing, the man brushed off the pastry, made the best of it, and lay back down for another dark interval.

The next day it was the same thing: the bell, the steward, the ceremoniously served dirty pastry!

"What's going on here?" he shouted. "I demand to see a menu! What nerve! Do you know who I am?"

"Yes, indeed," answered the stoic steward. "You are the man who, in his lifetime, always made sure that his own needs were met. You were stingy with family, friends, and servants. In fact, that made it difficult for us to prepare for you. Do you remember that last banquet, when a poor man knocked at your door? He begged for food, but you didn't find it in your heart to have him fed in the kitchen. No, you just tossed him one meager pastry that had been dropped and stepped on. It is that very fare that you yourself are now being served. It is all you gave us to work with. It's only what you give away that lasts, you know."

For this man, like the rich man in the story of Lazarus the beggar, it was too late. His barns and houses back on earth may have been full. But his store of generosity was empty.

It's relatively easy to give away what we don't need or value anyway. But this parable says to me that nurturing our own soul necessarily involves caring for others. It is in self-forgetfulness, when we are simply planting and sowing and building and saving and restoring for those who will reap after us, that we reflect something of the economy of heaven.

—ISABEL ANDERS IN *SOUL MOMENTS: TIMES WHEN HEAVEN TOUCHES EARTH*

I cannot promise you a life of sunshine;
I cannot promise riches, wealth, or gold;
I cannot promise you an easy pathway
That leads away from change or growing old.

But I can promise all my heart's devotion;
A smile to chase away your tears of sorrow;
A love that's ever true and ever growing;
A hand to hold in yours through each tomorrow.

—AUTHOR UNKNOWN

I wonder…do you remember
Our very first quarrel?
We were sitting at the table
Before a dinner of leftovers.
Teasingly, you took the first bite
Without expressing thanks.
When I asked why, you said,
"Honey, it's all been blessed before."

—RUTH HARMS CALKIN IN *HOLD ME CLOSE*

Come, my Way, my Truth, my Life:
Such a Way, as gives us breath:
Such a Truth, as ends all strife:
Such a Life, as killeth death.

Come, my Light, my Feast, my Strength:
Such a Light, as shows a feast:
Such a Feast, as mends in length:
Such a Strength, as makes his guest.

Come, my Joy, my Love, my Heart:
Such a Joy, as none can move:
Such a Love, as none can part:
Such a Heart, as joys in love.

—"THE CALL" BY GEORGE HERBERT (1593–1633)

The quality of mercy is not strain'd,
It droppeth as the gentle rain from heaven
Upon the place beneath: it is twice blest;
It blesseth him that gives and him that takes:
'Tis mightiest in the mightiest: it becomes
The throned monarch better than his crown;…
It is enthroned in the hearts of kings,
It is an attribute to God himself;
And earthly power doth then show likest God's
When mercy seasons justice.

—PORTIA, IN SHAKESPEARE'S *MERCHANT OF VENICE*

The state of marriage is one that requires more virtue and constancy than any other. It is a perpetual exercise of mortification.

—SAINT FRANCIS DE SALES (1567–1622)

May God relieve the wants of others and give us thankful hearts; for Christ's sake.

JOHN DALLAS, QUOTED IN *SHORT PRAYERS FOR THE LONG DAY*, COMPILED BY GILES AND MELVILLE HARCOURT

Jesus would give up everything of this world before he left it. He exercised the most perfect poverty. Even when he left the holy house of Nazareth and went out to preach, he had nowhere to lay his head. He lived on the poorest food, and on what was given to him by those who loved and served him. And therefore he chose a death in which not even his clothes were left to him. He parted with what seemed most necessary, and even a part of him, by the law of human nature since the Fall.

Grant us in like manner, O dear Lord, to care nothing for anything on earth, and to bear the loss of all things, and to endure even shame, reproach, contempt and mockery, rather than that you shall be ashamed of us at the last day.

—BLESSED JOHN HENRY CARDINAL NEWMAN

Honor, riches, marriage-blessing,
Long continuance, and increasing,
Hourly joys be still upon you!

—SHAKESPEARE IN *THE TEMPEST*, ACT IV, SCENE 1

IS WEALTH GOOD?

According to noted financial author Larry Burkett, communicating about money in marriage is either the best or the worst area of communication in the relationship.

By wisdom wealth is won;
But riches purchased wisdom yet for none.

—BAYARD TAYLOR

The story is told of a Jewish sage who understood the deep truth that all things ultimately belong to God. A beggar once approached the sage with his hands held out for food. The wise man asked him what he usually ate. The poor man replied, "Fatted chicken and aged wine." The sage reprimanded the beggar for expecting such rich food that might deplete the resources of the community. The man responded, "Do I eat what is theirs? No. I consume what is God's."

Bless us, gracious Lord,
Bless this food, set before us,
Bless those who have prepared it
And give bread to those who have none.
To God who gives our daily bread
A thankful song we raise,
And pray that he who sends us food
May fill our hearts with praise.

—THOMAS TALLIS (1505–1585)

Lord, this very day
This very hour
My husband and I
Have come face-to-face
With a wrenching crisis.
Our work has folded
Our finances are depleted
Our ambitious plans have exploded
Our glistening dreams are smashed.
We don't know where to turn—
Or scarcely how to pray.
Yet your Word tells us
There is not a single catastrophe
No matter how staggering
No matter how shattering
That we may not bring to You.
It isn't only that we may—
You tell us that we must.
Dear God of Promises
You are never lost in our mysteries.
Our eyes are turned toward You.
Keep us from looking back.
While we wait with bleeding hearts
Remind us again, and yet again
That our absence of happiness
Does not mean the absence of God.

—RUTH HARMS CALKIN IN *HOLD ME CLOSE*

Questions for Further Reflection

1. How have financially difficult times affected your relationship as spouses, and what have you learned from them?

2. What proportion of your happiness is connected to the status of your wealth or possessions? How would you like these percentages to change in relation to family times, degree of dedication to God's work, and other values?

3. What advice would you give a newly married couple about the importance of finances in the context of long-term Christian marriage?

4. In your minds, how closely is personal value connected with monetary strength? How does the biblical view of wealth affect this estimation?

Through the Valley

"In sickness
and in health"

For I am convinced that neither death, nor life, nor angels, nor rulers, nor things present, nor things to come, nor powers, nor height, nor depth, nor anything else in all creation, will be able to separate us from the love of God in Christ Jesus our Lord.

—ROMANS 8:38–39

Bless thy servant (my wife or husband) with health of body and of spirit. Let the hand of thy blessing be upon his/her head, night and day, and support her in all necessities, strengthen him in all temptations, comfort her in all her sorrows, and let him/her be thy servant in all changes; and make us both to dwell with thee for ever in thy favor, in the light of thy countenance, and in thy glory.

—FROM JEREMY TAYLOR (1613–1667)

A disciple asked a learned rabbi why God used to speak directly to the people but never does so today. The wise man replied, "People cannot *bend low enough* now to hear what God says."

In a marriage partnership, as in all sacred relationships, it is essential to remember humility of spirit, to live close to the supporting ground of our marriage vows, and to remember to bend low enough to hear the wailing of a needy world—to which we can perhaps contribute our love and care as a church, a family, a community. From such a position, we are more likely to find solidarity with God's people around us.

It is certainly true that when things are going well, we are less likely to seek God's voice; we do not look for the same assurances and help as when we are going through the valley—of hardship, stress, or sometimes illness and disease.

It often takes a physical catastrophe to awaken us to our human plight of battling for life—shared by so many in various ways over the course of a lifetime.

Studies show that the promise of "in sickness and in health" offers different odds as to likely fulfillment by women over men in marriage. In *Cancer* journal (November 15, 2009), two neurooncologists, Marc Chamberlain and Michael Glanz, report that out of 515 married patients with severe symptoms of multiple sclerosis or cancer, the overall separation or divorce rate was 11.6 percent. That figure does not reflect a great difference from the number of divorces in a similar sampling of nonpatients. The study showed, however, that the patient was six times more likely to be a woman when such a break in relationship—what the researchers called "partner abandonment"—occurred. In marriages in which women were the diagnosed partner, 20.8 percent ended in separation or divorce. In marriages in which men were the diagnosed partner, it was 2.9 percent.

The researchers further commented that some studies suggest men are less capable of taking on a caregiving role and assuming the burdens of home and family maintenance. Thus women become willing sooner to commit to the burdens of having a sick spouse. Of course, every case is different.

"In sickness and in health" should apply equally to both partners. Although it may not be easy to see how the care-giving partner will also benefit from a commitment that withstands another's pain and suffering, it is clearly an integral part of the marriage vow "for all the days of our lives"—even those days in which the balance of misery seems to far outweigh the joy of unity and love.

Of course, the best approach to potentially facing "the valley of the shadow" that is prolonged illness is to already be living in mature commitment and praying together daily for each other's health in mind, body, and spirit. This is the essence of love: desiring the best for the other as well as for oneself, always envisioning and working within the broader context of relationship that overshadows what I want or what works for me.

Plato wrote, "Perfect wisdom has four parts: wisdom, the principle of doing things aright; justice, the principle of doing things equally in public and private; fortitude, the principle of not fleeing danger, but meeting it; and temperance, the principle of subduing desires and living moderately."

And Jesus' message in John 13:34 concerning God's standards for love and commitment is clear: "I give you a new commandment, that you love one another. Just as I have loved you, you also should love one another."

There is perhaps no greater opportunity to "be Christ" to each other than in the straits of disability, pain, or addiction—as illustrated in the following vignette:

> Michael's alcoholism didn't exhibit the usual signs. He didn't lose his job or get arrested for driving under the influence. When Michael entered treatment in 1995, however, he knew that his marriage and family hung in the balance.

When Michael married Peggy in 1974, dealing with alcoholism wasn't in their plan. For Peggy, the illness was cruelly ironic, since her family has a history of alcoholism. She later confided to Michael that of all the illnesses they could have faced—even cancer—alcoholism was last on the list. No one chooses to have cancer, but many people think that addiction results from a personal choice rather than a disease.

Despite the possible risks to his marriage, Michael had reached the point "where you need to be rigorously honest." He needed to admit his own brokenness to Peggy, despite his feelings of shame, remorse, and helplessness. He took a risk, with no guarantee that Peggy would support him.

The ordeal has made them stronger. Peggy learned to deal with Michael's illness with help from counseling and close friends. Two years ago, Michael completed a master's program in counseling psychology and works with individuals and families who are dealing with addictions.

Michael likes to quote Jim Wallis, editor of *Sojourners,* who says, "Hope is believing in spite of the evidence and then watching the evidence change." Michael and Peggy believed even when their marriage received a shock that neither had foreseen. They also know that through it all, "God was doing for them what they could not have done for themselves."

—FROM THE UNITED STATES CONFERENCE OF CATHOLIC BISHOPS IN
"NOT WHAT WE PLANNED"

Thoughts, Prayers, and Blessings

O Lord, in Whom is our hope, remove far from us, we pray Thee, empty hopes and presumptuous confidence. Make our hearts so right with Thy most holy and loving heart, that hoping in Thee we may do good; until that day when faith and hope shall be abolished by sight and possession, and love shall be all in all.

—CHRISTINA G. ROSSETTI (1830–1894)

The prayer of faith will save the sick, and the Lord will raise them up; and anyone who has committed sins will be forgiven. Therefore confess your sins to one another, and pray for one another, so that you may be healed. The prayer of the righteous is powerful and effective.

—JAMES 5:15–16

Gracious Lord, whose will is human well-being in its totality, open our hearts and minds to receive your never-failing love, that we may know the healing power of Jesus Christ, and be made well in mind, body, and spirit, in the peace of the Holy Spirit, who lives and reigns with you in glory everlasting. Amen.

—*UNDERSTANDING THE SUNDAY SCRIPTURES, YEAR B*

Saint Jude Thaddeus is the patron saint of impossible causes. We turn to Saint Jude in times of despair and seemingly hopeless causes, including depression, grief, unemployment, and sickness.

His surname, Thaddeus, means "generous," "courageous," "kind." Our Lord told Saint Bridget of Sweden, "He will show himself most willing to give help."

Saint Jude is traditionally depicted carrying the image of Jesus in his hand. This represents the imprint of the divine Countenance entrusted to him by Jesus.

ISABEL ANDERS

PRAYER IN TIME OF ILLNESS:

Lord Jesus, you came into the world to heal our infirmities and to endure our sufferings. You went about healing all and bringing comfort to those in pain and need. We come before you now in this time of illness, asking that you may be the source of our strength in body, courage in spirit and patience in pain. May we join ourselves more closely to you on the cross and in your suffering that through them we may draw our patience and hope. Assist us and restore us to health so that united more closely to your family, the Church, we may give praise and honor to your name. Amen.

He is the half part of a blessed man,
Left to be finished by such as she;
And she a fair divided excellence,
Whose fullness of perfection lies in him.
O, two such silver currents, when they join,
Do glorify the banks that bound them in.

—SHAKESPEARE: FIRST CITIZEN IN *KING JOHN*, ACT II, SCENE 1

PSALM OF COMFORT:

As a deer longs for flowing streams,
so my soul longs for you, O God.
My soul thirsts for God,
for the living God.
When shall I come and behold
the face of God?
My tears have been my food
day and night,
while people say to me continually,
"Where is your God?"

These things I remember,
as I pour out my soul:
how I went with the throng,
and led them in procession to the house of God,
with glad shouts and songs of thanksgiving,
a multitude keeping festival.
Why are you cast down, O my soul,
and why are you disquieted within me?
Hope in God; for I shall again praise him,
my help and my God.

—PSALM 42:1–5

In our discussions about marriage, we made it a point to ask couples about the difficult periods in their relationship. What were the most difficult times? How did they deal with those times? What did they learn from having struggled through those times together? Most of what couples shared with us centered around what we call "land-mine emotions": explosive feelings or attitudes that have the ability to do great damage to a relationship.

Carolyn, married twelve years, captures the idea behind this concept. "Remember the statement from the comic strip *Pogo*, 'We have met the enemy, and he is us'? On their wedding day, every couple should be reminded of that statement, because it is especially true of marriage." Looking back over her own marriage, Carolyn considers where the greatest challenges came from. "Generally, the greatest threat to a marriage doesn't come from outside the marriage, but from within. Each of us brings our unique emotional makeup to a relationship, and it can work for or against a couple. Believe me, if you don't learn to control your feelings, it won't be long and they will start controlling you. Then, when they decide to break loose, it's just like having a bucking bronco in your living room—and when it's all over, there's an awful lot of debris and a lot of things that will need fixing."

…In our own marriage, we have found that certain forms of ritual help us express and receive forgiveness, and thus heal and grow. For example, a genuine statement of "I'm sorry," followed by a kiss, will be enough. At other times, we might just offer our hand as a gesture of reconciliation. We also find that praying together, especially the Lord's Prayer, emphasizes our willingness to forgive and be forgiven.

Writing is also effective. If something serious has damaged our sense of closeness as a couple, we turn to the visual word. We write down the hurt on a piece of paper and then together burn it in some way, letting the flame represent the healing light of Christ and the need to keep the flame of love alive in our marriage.

—WILLIAM E. RABIOR AND SUSAN C. RABIOR IN
9 WAYS TO NURTURE YOUR MARRIAGE

I know not, O my God, what may befall me today, but I am well convinced that nothing will happen which thou has not foreseen and ordained from eternity. I adore thy eternal and impenetrable designs, I submit to them for thy love. I sacrifice myself in union with the sacrifice of Jesus Christ my divine Savior, I ask in his holy name for patience and resignation in my sufferings, and perfect conformity of my will to thine in all things, past, present and to come.

My God, I have nothing worthy of thy acceptance to offer thee, I know nothing, I have but one heart to give thee: I may be deprived of health, reputation and even life, but my heart is my own. I consecrate it to thee, hoping never to resume it and desiring not to live if not for thee. Amen.

—ELIZABETH OF FRANCE (1764–1794), SISTER TO LOUIS XVI

I believe that you become married—truly married—slowly, over time, through all the road-rage incidents and precolonoscopy enemas, all the small and large moments that you never expected to happen and certainly didn't plan to endure. But then you do: you endure.

I had been viewing our marriage like the waves on the ocean, a fact of life, determined by the sandbars below, shaped by fate and the universe, not by me.

…The "good-enough marriage" is characterized by its capacity to allow spouses to keep growing, to afford them the strength and bravery required to face the world.

In the end, I settled on this vision of marriage, felt the logic of applying myself to it. Maybe the perversity we all feel in the idea of striving at marriage—the reason so few of us do it—stems from a misapprehension of the proper goal. In the early years, we take our marriages to be vehicles for wish fulfillment: we get the mate, maybe even a house, an end to loneliness, some kids. But to keep expecting our marriages to fulfill our desires—to bring us the unending happiness or passion or intimacy or stability we crave—and to measure our unions by their capacity to satisfy those longings, is naive, even demeaning.

—ELIZABETH WEIL IN "MARRIED (HAPPILY) WITH ISSUES,"
THE NEW YORK TIMES MAGAZINE

Marriage has three blessings. The first is children, to be received and raised for God's service. The second is the loyal faithfulness by which each serves the other. The third is the sacrament of matrimony, which signifies the inseparable union of Christ with His Church.

—SAINT THOMAS AQUINAS

God be in my head,
and in my understanding;
God be in my eyes,
and in my looking;
God be in my mouth,
and in my speaking;
God be in my heart,
and in my thinking;
God be at my end,
and at my departing.
Amen.

—The Sarum Primer, 1558

Eternal Light, shine into our hearts;
Eternal Goodness, deliver us from evil;
Eternal Power, be our support;
Eternal Wisdom, scatter the darkness of our ignorance;
Eternal Pity, have mercy on us;
that with all our heart and mind and soul and strength
we may seek your face
and be brought by your infinite mercy
into your holy presence;
through Jesus Christ our Lord.

—Blessed Alcuin of York (c. 730–804)

God, there are some years
We would like to cross off the calendar.
This is one of those years.
From January to December my husband and I
Have felt like wounded soldiers
Fighting a losing battle.
Hospitals, life-threatening illness
Surgeries, financial drain, pain
A family death, grief, anxiety
Night-tossing, weariness, silent tears.
Other things, too:
A flooded patio, pieces of roofing
Scattered by howling winds
Two car accidents in bumper-to-bumper traffic
Dwindling hope, thundering doubts
The fear-stabbing question
"Lord, don't You love us anymore?"

And yet, dear God
How dare we deny Your day-by-day comfort
At times when we needed it most.
Phone calls bringing encouragement
Notes in the mail
Delicious meals lovingly prepared by friends
A paragraph in a book renewing our trust
Your Word bringing light in the darkness
A sparrow's song during drizzling rain
Your whispered words to our hearts:
"When the pain stays, I stay, too."

O God, You have been our high tower
You have been our hiding place
You have been our sure defense.
The hymn of the psalmist is our hymn, too:
"I will bless the holy Name of God
And not forget the glorious things He does."
Over this year's calendar we will finally write
"Surely the Lord was in this place
Though we knew it not."

—RUTH HARMS CALKIN IN *HOLD ME CLOSE*

Let me not to the marriage of true minds
Admit impediments. Love is not love
Which alters when it alteration finds,
Or bends with the remover to remove.
O no! it is an ever fixed mark
That looks on tempests and is never shaken;
It is the star to every wandering bark,
Whose worth's unknown, although his height be taken.
Love's not Time's fool, though rosy lips and cheeks
Within his bending sickle's compass come;
Love alters not with his brief hours and weeks,
But bears it out even to the edge of doom.
If this be error and upon me proved,
I never writ, nor no man ever loved.

—SHAKESPEARE, SONNET 116

Lord
We're so weary tonight
My husband and I.
Please rest us!
We're thirsty.
Give us Living Water!
We've fallen flat
On our faces.
Pick us up!
We're tired of trying
To maintain the "image."
Let us see You!
Right now
We'd like very much to give up.
Hold us very close!

—RUTH HARMS CALKIN IN *HOLD ME CLOSE*

Thank you, Lord:
For being our Strength and our Shield,
at times when the cold winds
and hard blows of outside forces—
the events around us of disruption and confusion—
could so easily
have pulled us apart.

Thank you for days of joy, of health and ease,
as well as for reminding us through
the inevitable pains of life
of our mortality, our age,
our frailty, our dependence, our humanness…

and of you
and your presence in our midst—
standing with us in power
and bestowing compassion in the face of our weakness.

Give us eyes to see and ears to hear
what is really happening to us and to
those around us.

Bless all those who are closely connected
to us by blood, through work, and
simply by dwelling among us in the human community.

Let us see and deeply acknowledge
how our lives are connected by bonds
of mystery and also of responsibility,
especially in your Church.
Let us learn ever more lovingly how
to minister to each other
in sickness and in health…
and thus fulfill the law of Christ.

For the "law" of Christ is love. Amen.

—ISABEL ANDERS

Questions for Further Reflection

1. When has a physical catastrophe such as an illness or accident or other condition threatened to separate you and challenged your commitment to unity? What is your family story of how you remained committed and together?

2. What are the biggest obstacles to overcome when illness intrudes on a family's peace? How does prayer address these difficulties and lead us to another level of understanding and acceptance?

3. What are your favorite Bible verses of comfort and healing that can be incorporated into your prayers together—and returned to often—as you remember how God has brought healing into your life in the past?

4. What have you learned spiritually from the challenge and experience of staying together faithfully "in sickness and in health"?

For All
Time

"All the days
of our lives"

Husbands should love their wives as they do their own bodies. He who loves his wife loves himself. For no one ever hates his own body, but he nourishes and tenderly cares for it, just as Christ does for the church, because we are members of his body.

—EPHESIANS 5:28–30

Grow old along with me!
The best is yet to be,
The last of life, for which the first was made:
Our times are in his hand…

—ROBERT BROWNING IN *RABBI BEN EZRA*
(FROM *DRAMATIS PERSONAE*, 1864)

You show me the path of life.
In your presence there is fullness of joy;
in your right hand are pleasures forevermore.

—PSALM 16:11

Opportunity is missed by most people because it is dressed in overalls and looks like work.

—THOMAS ALVA EDISON

True love is delicate and kind, full of gentle perception and understanding, full of beauty and grace, full of joy unutterable. There should be some flavor of this in all our love for others. We are all one. We are one flesh in the Mystical Body as man and woman are said to be one flesh in marriage. With such a love one would see all things new; we would begin to see people as they really are, as God sees them.

—DOROTHY DAY

W e cannot be fully human without one another and the relationships we build in this life. We cannot be one in the body of Christ without enduring love and acceptance of our differences. And we cannot sustain the unity of the marriage relationship unless we are willing to become adults: to commit ourselves as deeply as we are able before God for the long term.

Doing so for "all the days of our lives" sounds, in turns, poetic, idealistic, frightening, unrealistic, even crazy—a blind acceptance of what we cannot imagine that may lie ahead. But in marriage, as with any commitment worth making, love has to be lived one day at a time—sometimes one moment at a time.

As we seek to discover the art of maintaining a growing, healthy, committed marriage, we can learn from those who are further along in the process—couples who have endured through the years and decades and have discovered along the way how to keep love alive.

In *Love's Journey: The Seasons and Stages of Relationship* Michael Gurian tells about a conversation he had with a woman on a talk show about the stages of relationship. Gurian and the host of the show had just asked to hear from couples whose happy, growing lives together had received a damaging shock in midstream.

"Your love will be tested, make no mistake," said Norma, a woman in her sixties. "You'll get everything just right. The slip-covers will be just right on the couches, and he'll have all the tools up in the garage, and your kids will be in ballet and basketball, and the walk is swept and the sprinkler system is in and things seem so clean, so orderly. And then boom! some huge hand scoops you all up and throws you around, and you fall back down in a terrible heap. If the two of you don't work together, you're sunk.

"It happened to us when our middle daughter got pregnant, at fifteen. Our world fell apart. It just fell apart. Eugene became an ogre, like he didn't love his own flesh and blood anymore. I hated him for that, but I knew he had his own worries. He said it was all my fault—she was a girl, I was supposed to be looking after her.

"That was his way. When he was mad at himself, he got mad at me. I just did my best to hold things together."

Gurian asked, "What happened? How did things work out?"

"Well, that was twenty years ago. We're still together. We've got five grandkids. We wouldn't trade them. You just go on. You just fight to hold things together. What else can you do?"

What else, indeed. Life tests us.

But as basic as *listening to each other* sounds, it is fair to say that such a practice is necessary *at the very least* for couples to find the unity to face—together—an increasingly complicated world. And as Christian partners, prayer that incorporates the practice of listening to God, worshiping together, and following the teachings of Scripture can add priceless layers of value and depth that will help to build up this love relationship from the ground floor.

Saint Irenaeus (c. 120–c. 202) gave this advice that is most appropriate for couples facing the future together:

"It is not you who shapes God, it is God who shapes you. If then you are the work of God, await the hand of the Artist who does all things in due season. Offer the Potter your heart, soft and tractable, and keep the form in which the Artist has fashioned you. Let your clay be moist, lest you grow hard and lose the imprint of the Potter's fingers."

To have reached mature years together in marriage is to have walked together with God and each other through many of the "either/ors" and "both/ands" of the marriage vows: "for better or worse"; "in good times and in bad"; "for richer and for poorer"; "in sickness and in health."

To look forward to a continued partnership in love means to pay attention to the little things; to be each other's strongest advocate; to avoid jumping to conclusions; to stay flexible in God's hands—and to rely on the power of God, the redeeming love of Christ, and the grace of the Holy Spirit in both belief and practice as you journey together.

Thoughts, Prayers, and Blessings

Lord, we are rivers running to thy sea,
Our waves and ripples all derived from thee:
A nothing we should have, a nothing be,
      Except for thee.

Sweet are the waters of thy shoreless sea,
Make sweet our waters that make haste to thee;
Pour in thy sweetness, that ourselves may be
      Sweetness to thee.

—CHRISTINA ROSSETTI (1830–1894)

Blessed are You, O Lord our God,
priest of mystical and pure marriage,
creator of the law of marriage of the body,
preserver of immortality, and provider
of the good things in life.

—BYZANTINE WEDDING LITURGY

Dearest Lord, please bless this couple
Whose lives have been joined today
Shine Your strength and will upon them
Be a light to guide their way
Sanctify them with Your valor
When they face the road ahead
So, their bond remains as sacred
As the moment they were wed.
Fill their lives with love and laughter
Shared with friends and family
On this day and each one after
From now 'til eternity
Guide their hearts by Your direction
Hold their souls in Your embrace
So they shall have the protection
Of Your everlasting grace.

Dearest Lord, please bless this union
Of two hearts, now joined as one
While they journey toward the future
On the path they have begun
Cast Your faith and might upon them
Mend their hearts, should they feel strife
So they shall remain forever
As loving husband and wife.

—"WEDDING PRAYER," BY POET JILL EISNAUGLE

If I speak in the tongues of mortals and of angels, but do not have love, I am a noisy gong or a clanging cymbal. And if I have prophetic powers, and understand all mysteries and all knowledge, and if I have all faith, so as to remove mountains, but do not have love, I am nothing. If I give away all my possessions, and if I hand over my body so that I may boast, but do not have love, I gain nothing.

Love is patient; love is kind; love is not envious or boastful or arrogant or rude. It does not insist on its own way; it is not irritable or resentful; it does not rejoice in wrongdoing, but rejoices in the truth. It bears all things, believes all things, hopes all things, endures all things.

Love never ends. But as for prophecies, they will come to an end; as for tongues, they will cease; as for knowledge, it will come to an end. For we know only in part, and we prophesy only in part; but when the complete comes, the partial will come to an end. When I was a child, I spoke like a child, I thought like a child, I reasoned like a child; when I became an adult, I put an end to childish ways. For now we see in a mirror, dimly, but then we will see face to face. Now I know only in part; then I will know fully, even as I have been fully known. And now faith, hope, and love abide, these three; and the greatest of these is love.

—1 CORINTHIANS 13

What I do
And what I dream include thee, as the wine
Must taste of its own grapes. And when I sue
God for myself, He hears that name of thine,
And sees within my eyes, the tears of two.

—ELIZABETH BARRETT BROWNING, FROM SONNET 6,
SONNETS FROM THE PORTUGUESE (1845–1846)

Bless this marriage, and grant to these Your servants a peaceful life, length of days, chastity, mutual love in the bond of peace, long-lived offspring, gratitude from their children, and a crown of glory that will not fade away. Fill their house with wheat, wine, oil, and every good thing, so that they may give in turn to those in need.

—BYZANTINE WEDDING LITURGY

EASTER, OUR MARRIAGE CEREMONY:

You have protected us, Jesus, from endless disaster.
You spread your hands over us like wings.
You poured your blood over the earth,
Because you loved us.
The anger which we deserved you turned away from us
And restored us to friendship with God.

The heavens may have your spirit, paradise your soul,
But the earth has your blood.
We celebrate the coming of your Spirit always:
The Spirit leads the mystic dance throughout the year,
But Easter comes and goes.
Power came from heaven to raise you from death,
So that we and all creatures could see you.
All living things gather round you at Easter.
There is joy, honor, celebration, delight.

The darkness of death is driven away.
Life is restored everywhere.
The gates of heaven are thrown open.
In you, risen Jesus, God has shown us himself,
So we can rise to him as gods.
The gates of hell are shattered.

In you, risen Jesus, those already dead rise to life,
Affirming the good news of eternal life.
Now your promise has been fulfilled.
Now the earth is singing and dancing
Easter is our marriage ceremony.

At Easter, dear Jesus, you make us your brides.
Sealing the union with your Spirit.
The great marriage hall is full of guests,
All dressed for the wedding.
No one is rejected for want of a wedding dress.
We come to you as spiritual virgins,
Our lamps are fresh and bright, with ample oil,
The light within our souls will never go out.
The fire of grace burns in us all.

We pray you, our sovereign Christ,
Stretch out your strong hands over your whole Church
And over all your faithful people.
Defend, protect, and preserve them,
Fight and do battle for them,
Subdue the invisible powers that oppose them.
Raise now the sign of victory over us
And grant that we may sing the song of triumph.
May you rule for ever and ever.

—SAINT HIPPOLYTUS (C. 190–C. 236)

O Lord, on this our wedding anniversary
we focus on the many blessings of our years together:
The sharing of the cup of sorrow and joy…
The blessings that have exceeded all hopes…
The oneness you have granted us in earthly flesh…
That together we are more than the sum of two persons…
That when we pray, our efforts are doubled…
And that you give us always the hope of
love multiplied further in the years to come,
by your grace.
Amen.

—ISABEL ANDERS

The six most important words in the world:
I ADMIT I MADE A MISTAKE.
The five most important words in the world:
YOU DID A GOOD JOB.
The three most important words in the world:
IF YOU PLEASE.
The two most important words in the world:
THANK YOU.
The most important word in the world:
WE.
The least important word in the world:
I.

—GILES AND MELVILLE HARCOURT IN *SHORT PRAYERS FOR THE LONG DAY*

For joys of service, thee we praise,
whose favor crowneth all our days;
For humble tasks that bring delight,
when done, O Lord, as in thy sight.
Accept our sufferings, Lord most high,
our work, our purpose sanctify,
and with our gifts may we have place,
now in the Kingdom of thy grace.

—SAINT VENANTIUS (530–609)

O Christ, the Vine with living Fruit,
The twelvefold-fruited Tree of Life,
The Balm in Gilead after strife,
The valley Lily and the Rose;
Stronger than Lebanon, Thou Root;
Sweeter than clustered grapes, Thou Vine;
O Best, Thou Vineyard of red wine,
Keeping thy best wine till the close.

Pearl of great price Thyself alone,
And ruddier than the ruby Thou;
Most precious lightning Jasper stone,
Head of the corner spurned before:
Fair Gate of pearl, Thyself the Door;
Clear golden Street, Thyself the Way;
By Thee we journey toward Thee now,
Through Thee shall enter Heaven one day.

—CHRISTINA ROSSETTI, FROM *"LYRA MESSIANICA,"* 1864

Where shall wisdom be found?
And where is the place of understanding?
Mortals do not know the way to it,
and it is not found in the land of the living.
The deep says, "It is not in me,"
and the sea says, "It is not with me."
It cannot be gotten for gold,
and silver cannot be weighed out as its price.
It cannot be valued in the gold of Ophir,
in precious onyx or sapphire.
Gold and glass cannot equal it,
nor can it be exchanged for jewels of fine gold.
No mention shall be made of coral or of crystal;
the price of wisdom is above pearls.
The chrysolite of Ethiopia cannot compare with it,
nor can it be valued in pure gold.
Where then does wisdom come from?
And where is the place of understanding?
It is hidden from the eyes of all living,
and concealed from the birds of the air.
Abaddon and Death say,
"We have heard a rumor of it with our ears."

God understands the way to it,
and he knows its place.
For he looks to the ends of the earth,
and sees everything under the heavens.
When he gave to the wind its weight,

and apportioned out the waters by measure;
when he made a decree for the rain,
and a way for the thunderbolt;
then he saw it and declared it;
he established it, and searched it out.
And he said to humankind,
"Truly, the fear of the Lord, that is wisdom;
and to depart from evil is understanding."

—JOB 28:12–28

"How do you and Father continue loving, through so many years of difficulty, toil and disappointments?" the Daughter asked.

"The dawning of love is like the morning, but its trajectory will take you through the lean years and the bleak and barren days," the Mother admitted. "Nevertheless, you hold onto Love for dear Life—for your own Destiny is defined in its folds."

—ISABEL ANDERS IN
BECOMING FLAME: UNCOMMON MOTHER-DAUGHTER WISDOM

"Abba Moses," asked Abba Sylvanus, "can a man lay a new foundation every day?"

The old man said, "If he works hard, he can lay a new foundation at every moment."

—*THE PARADISE OF THE FATHERS*

An adventure is only an inconvenience rightly considered. An inconvenience is only an adventure wrongly considered.

—G.K. CHESTERTON

Uphold me according to your promise, that I may live.

—PSALM 119:116

Contrasts—night and day, siege and deliverance, imprisonment and glorious freedom—are reminders that weeping may linger for the night, but joy comes with the morning. The story goes on and on…the one we've been cast in. And *anything* can pop out at us, just around the bend.

The bad news for the soul is that we're never totally "out of the woods" in this life. The good news is that *this is what life is*: the trekking on, the courage, the doubts, the stamina, the occasional blindness, the willingness to ask for help as we need it on the way.

"I will be with them in trouble" (Psalm 91:15). An appropriate petition to carry in our hearts for the journey has also been phrased by saints of the past as simply, "Lord, have mercy!" As a soul prayer, it is a one-size-fits-all-occasions refrain. Don't leave home without it.

—ISABEL ANDERS IN SOUL MOMENTS: TIMES WHEN HEAVEN TOUCHES EARTH

Gracious God, families come in many shapes and sizes. Some consist of a single person. Some are made up of many diverse personalities. We ask your blessing on all families. Regardless of size, families long for unity with you, their Creator, your Son Jesus, their Redeemer, and your Holy Spirit. Grant them the grace to seek you and to be found by you and to live forever in the joy of your kingdom. Amen.

—AUTHOR UNKNOWN

As the family goes, so goes the nation and so goes the whole world in which we live.

—POPE JOHN PAUL II

Contrary to the popular sentiment, marriages are not made in heaven. Rather, lasting and satisfying marriages are built by imperfect and finite human beings, little by little, day by day, here on Earth.

Those who are married—newlyweds as well as those married for many decades—know that we can always do something more, try a little harder, stretch ourselves a little farther, to improve the quality of our marriage. Positive changes in a marriage will not happen unless we want them, will them, and work for them.

...It's been said that a wedding lasts only one day, but a marriage lasts a lifetime. May you know newlywed joy throughout your lifetime together.

—WILLIAM E. RABIOR AND SUSAN C. RABIOR IN
9 WAYS TO NURTURE YOUR MARRIAGE

I like only one definition of "develops":
to unfold.
It suggests fluidity,
lack of force,
natural discovery,
a rock rolling downhill,
not a boulder unloosed
by a catapult,
just a promise: "to be continued."

—DIANE M. MOORE IN *A MOMENT SEIZED*

God's way, love of neighbor as self, seems to be a process that has everything to do with our own salvation, the embracing of our humanness that is the focal point of being redeemable creatures. It is only as we are realistic about ourselves, before God, that we have anything to offer others. I find increasingly that the way I treat myself as God's child, stumbling through life day to day, has much more to do with potential love of God and neighbor than I had ever thought.

—ISABEL ANDERS IN *THE FACES OF FRIENDSHIP*

Come, Holy Ghost, with God the Son
And God the Father, ever one;
Shed forth thy grace within our breast
And dwell with us a ready guest.

By every power, by heart and tongue,
By act and deed, thy praise be sung;
Inflame with perfect love each sense
That others' souls may kindle thence.

O Father, that we ask be done,
Through Jesus Christ, thine only Son;
Who, with the Holy Ghost and thee,
Doth live and reign eternally. Amen.

—ATTRIBUTED TO AMBROSE OF MILAN (340–397)

Questions for Further Reflection

1. What have been the turning points in your marriage that have brought you to greater unity or challenged the basis of your oneness in significant ways?

2. What day-to-day practices have you discovered that show respect for each other and make oneness more possible?

3. How has your prayer life as a couple contributed to your unity on a spiritual level over the years and helped to keep you together in love?

4. Discuss or draw some of the symbols or images that represent to you both the Christian life and the way of partnership in marriage. Suggestions: a tree, the cross, a bridge, a harvest field, Easter (as in the Hippolytus prayer quoted earlier), a rainbow, a rocky path, a yoke, a ladder, an open sky. Talk together about what these images mean to you personally.

Afterword

I am not an optimist, because I am not sure that everything ends well. Nor am I a pessimist because I am not sure everything ends badly. I just carry hope in my heart.
—VÁCLAV HAVEL

We can read the Psalms as a mirror of the soul, a reflection of the weather of doubt and fear and death, as well as God's answers to the ancient poet(s), promising joy and restoration and peace and life everlasting. When approaching the Bible, however, one might need to heed the warning, "Rough weather ahead!" This journey is not for the faint-hearted, the weak-souled. But the sustenance that will be provided is genuine meat and drink; or, to change the metaphor, amazing healing and calming of our troubled waters.

The secret and the key is that we can't really experience this until we willingly enter in.
—ISABEL ANDERS IN *SOUL MOMENTS: TIMES WHEN HEAVEN TOUCHES EARTH*

It may seem that this has been an impossible task, to seek to convey in these pages the essence of "marriage in the Christian faith and tradition"—a beautiful concept of metaphysical unity and spiritual solidarity. Not only is "marriage" in the abstract impossible to describe; attempting to point to an ideal can serve to set the reality of people's struggling lives in even harsher perspective.

And where to begin? What essentials to point to? What to leave out? How to allow for individuality, for mystery? were questions that came up throughout.

But I remembered that Emily Dickinson advised, "Tell all the Truth but tell it slant / Success in Circuit lies..." And so I offer these various perspectives and clusters of quotes and admonitions, prayers and voices—as a way of coming at this topic "on the slant."

Let me explain. As an author, looking straight-on at marriage is too limiting—though, like the blind men describing the elephant, one can walk around it and touch on various aspects of it, describe what it is not, and point to biblical principles that clearly apply both to the Christian life itself and to the relationship of partners in love and in Christ.

Of course, no one can live up to all the dimensions of the vows and promises treated here. Yet without the enlightenment of Scripture, the sacramental nature and unparalleled opportunity of sharing life with one's marriage partner, and the goal of loving each other as Christ has loved us—we would be in even harsher circumstances.

The reason for the many perspectives, points of view, and various experiences recounted in these pages is the simple truth that we only experience marriage as embodied people, in particularity; and we must observe, for admonition, its effects on the lives of those who choose to live within its "bounds."

Because we can't escape the element of human will, of choice, no true marriage can exist or continue without a certain freedom of response, of attitude, of a spiritual assent to the union that is the core of an ongoing relationship. What Christian marriage offers—and what mutual prayer and heart-sharing pave the way for and serve to accomplish—is a way of understanding and (as best as possible) of keeping our vows... valuing faithfulness as we also aim toward the other Christian virtues Christ has commended to us, with God's help.

I could not write about any of this without carrying hope and faith in my own heart—in spite of people who disappoint, situations that test our mettle to the nth degree—and always the shadow of our human fallenness as we crash into one another's wills and desires. It takes heart and soul and all that we can be together (for all our days) to affirm Christian marriage as a way of servanthood, a vocation among other callings, in a world that appears to be falling apart at the seams.

No one, in marriage or outside it—or in other relationships or situations—can do more than to bring Christ into the relationship, holding each other in God's love in the moment. Often the awareness of our commitment, the blessed fact of our union, even when we don't feel it, can hold us...until our own sense of love can be restored to us as feeling, as reality, as "glue"—and as a path that can bring us to the next stage, the next level of understanding, and whatever may lie ahead.

This experience, of course, comes in different shades and flavors for everyone. And so I have collected here many stories, anecdotes, images, and prayers as a montage or tapestry of "marriage enfleshed" (while adding my own sensibilities to the mix). Thus I offer this book to those who, with me, wish to celebrate their love with their spouse. And I hope they will also perceive, along with the suggestions of discipline in these pages, a spirit of heavenly lightness and even of the humor that is so much a part of my own marriage.

And so this book, along with various approaches to Bible study and prayer, can present an opportunity to remember points at which God has ministered to you as a family, as a couple, as an individual.

It is my prayer that *Blessings and Prayers for Married Couples: A Faith Full Love* enable readers to select from and be prompted by its passages—both to remember and to reimagine a life of trusting in God together. May your marriages be the shining out of a flame of belief and light to a darkened world. This is my offering of hope.

Acknowledgments

Isabel Anders, *Awaiting the Child: An Advent Journal* (Cambridge, MA: Cowley Publications, 1987, 2005), pp. 107–111. Used by permission.

Isabel Anders, *Becoming Flame: Uncommon Mother-Daughter Wisdom* (Eugene, OR: Wipf and Stock, 2010), pp. 45, 46. Used by permission.

Isabel Anders, *Soul Moments: Times When Heaven Touches Earth* (Cambridge, MA: Cowley Publications, 2006), pp. 18, 24-25, 54-55. Used by permission.

Isabel Anders, *The Faces of Friendship* (Eugene, OR: Wipf and Stock, 2008), p. 2. Used by permission of author and publisher.

St. Thomas Aquinas quote on p. 60 is from *Manual of Prayers,* compiled by Rev. James D. Watkins (*Our Sunday Visitor,* 1998).

W. H. Auden, *A Certain World: A Commonplace Book*, excerpt used by permission of The Wylie Agency LLC.

Renee Bartkowski, *Prayers for Married Couples* (Liguori, MO: Liguori, 1989). Excerpts used by permission.

John E. Biersdorf, *Healing of Purpose* (Nashville, TN: Abingdon, 1985), p. 186. Excerpt used by permission.

Avery Brooke, *Plain Prayers in a Complicated World* (Boston, MA: Cowley Publications, 1993), p. 119. Copyright © 1993 by Avery Brooke. Excerpt used by permission of Rowman & Littlefield, Lanham, MD.

Ruth Harms Calkin, *Hold Me Close: Prayer-Poems that Celebrate Married Love* (Wheaton, IL: Tyndale House Publishers, 1996), pp. 50, 68, 77, 78 79, 90, 91. Used by permission of author.

English translation of the *Catechism of the Catholic Church* for the United States of America (¶170), copyright © 1994, United States Catholic Conference, Inc.—Libreria Editrice Vaticana. English translation of the *Catechism of the Catholic Church: Modifications from the Editio Typica* copyright © 1997, United States Catholic Conference, Inc.—Libreria Editrice Vaticana.

G.K. Chesterton, excerpt from "On Running After One's Hat" in *All Things Considered,* 1908.

Dorothy Day, *On Pilgrimage* (Grand Rapids, MI: Wm. B. Eerdmans, 1999), pp. 239–40.

John S. Dunne, *The Reasons of the Heart: A Journey into Solitude and Back Again into the Human Circle* (Notre Dame, IN: University of Notre Dame Press, 1979), p. 141. Copyright © 1978 by John S. Dunne. Excerpt used by permission of publisher.

Jill Eisnaugle, poem entitled "Wedding Prayer," copyright © 2006 by Jill Eisnaugle. All rights reserved. Used by permission. See www.authorsden.com/jillaeisnaugle.

St. Francis de Sales quote is from Michael Hollings, ed., *A Thirst for God: Daily Readings with St. Francis de Sales* (London: Darton Longman & Todd, 1985).

Michael Gurian, *Love's Journey: The Seasons and Stages of Relationship* (Boston and London: Shambhala, 1995) pp. 203–04. Excerpt used by permission.

Giles and Melville Harcourt, compilers, *Short Prayers for the Long Day* (Liguori, MO: Triumph Books, 1996), pp. 56–57, 105, 111, 199. Used by permission.

Hildegard of Bingen quote is from *Analecta Sacra*, Vol. 8, ed. J. B. Pitra, transl. J. Cumming (Monte Cassino, 1882), p. 400.

St. Ignatius of Antioch translated quote on p. 9 is from *Ancient Christian Writers: The Epistles of St. Clement of Rome and St. Ignatius of Antioch* (New York: Newman Press and Paulist Press). Copyright © 1946 by Rev. Johannes Quasten and Rev. Joseph C. Plumpe.

English translation of *The Roman Missal* © 1973, International Committee on English in the Liturgy, Inc. (ICEL). Used by permission. (Wedding prayer on p. 6.)

Thomas á Kempis, *The Imitation of Christ* (Mineola, NY: Dover 2003). Used by permission.

Diane M. Moore, *A Moment Seized* (New Iberia, LA: Border Press, 2006), p. 9. Excerpt used by permission of the poet.

New American Bible with Revised New Testament and Revised Psalms © 1991, 1986, 1970 Confraternity of Christian Doctrine, Washington, D.C. Excerpt used by permission of the copyright owner. All Rights Reserved.

John Henry Cardinal Newman, *Meditations and Devotions of the Late Cardinal Newman*, 3rd. Ed. (London: Longmans, Green & Co., 1894).

H. King Oehmig, *Synthesis* (February 21, 2010). Excerpt used by permission.

The Psalm 85 adaptation on p. 77 is quoted from *The Book of Catholic Prayer* (Chicago: Loyola Press, 2000), pp. 219–220. © 1998 Seán Finnegan.

William E. Rabior and Susan C. Rabior, *9 Ways to Nurture Your Marriage* (Liguori, MO: Liguori, 2000), pp. 4, 27–28, 55, 78, 80. Used by permission.

Archbishop Fulton Sheen, *Three to Get Married* (New York: Appleton-Century-Crofts, 1951). Used by permission of Society for the Propagation of the Faith.

"Not What We Planned," copyright © 2010 USCCB Publishing; http://foryourmarriage.org/not-what-we-planned/. Excerpt used by permission.

Understanding the Sunday Scriptures, Year B (Chattanooga, TN: Read Mark Press, 2008), pp. 106, 136. Used by permission of publisher.

Vatican documents: Message of Pope Benedict XVI for the Celebration of the World Day of Peace, January 1, 2008; Message of Pope John XXIII; Messages of Pope John Paul II; Prayer from the *Book of Blessings* by The Congregation for Divine Worship. All used by permission of the copyright holder, Libreria Editrice Vaticana.

Elizabeth Weil, "Married (Happily) with Issues," *The New York Times Magazine*, December 6, 2009. Excerpt used by permission of author.

Simone Weil, *Letter to a Priest* (New York: Penguin, 2003). Excerpt used by permission of publisher.

Christopher West, *Theology of the Body*. Copyright © 2008 by Christopher West. All rights reserved. Excerpt used by permission of Ascension Press, West Chester, Pennsylvania.